Evaluating Digital Sources in Journalism

Building on a rich journalistic tradition of critical source analysis, this book considers the impact of the move from analogue to digital sources on information quality and presents methods and tools to verify information found online and help counter the spread of misinformation.

Evaluating Digital Sources in Journalism critically maps the prevalence of online manipulation, particularly images and videos from social media platforms, and considers the tools needed both to carry out and to counter this. Strategies are proposed to help readers evaluate content, context and sources, and ultimately build a foundation for carrying out their own online open-source investigations. The author brings together theories and best practices from a broad range of literature, including modern Scandinavian research on the concept of "source criticism", journalism and technology studies, advanced forensic verification research, and literature designed for practitioners, including blogs and industry publications.

Evaluating Digital Sources in Journalism is recommended reading for advanced journalism students and journalism practitioners.

Ståle Grut is a Doctoral Research Fellow at the University of Oslo's Department of Media and Communication. He spent close to a decade at the Norwegian public broadcasting's R&D lab, NRKbeta, as a strategic advisor and journalist covering new media. Grut has also served as an advisor at the Tinius Trust, controlling the largest shareholding of Schibsted Media Group, and as a board member of the Norwegian Online News Association.

Routledge Focus on Journalism Studies

Election Politics and the Mass Press in Long Edwardian Britain
Christopher Shoop-Worrall

Peripheral Actors in Journalism
Deviating from the Norm?
Aljosha Karim Schapals

Journalism's Racial Reckoning
The News Media's Pivot to Diversity and Inclusion
Brad Clark

Re-examining the UK Newspaper Industry
Marc Edge

Undercover Reporting, Deception, and Betrayal in Journalism
Denis Muller and Andrea Carson

Nonverbal Neutrality of Broadcasters Covering Crisis
Not Just What You Say But How You Say It
Danielle Deavours

Evaluating Digital Sources in Journalism
An Introduction to Digital Source Criticism
Ståle Grut

For more information about this series, please visit: www.routledge.com/Routledge-Focus-on-Journalism-Studies/book-series/RFJS

Evaluating Digital Sources in Journalism

An Introduction to Digital Source Criticism

Ståle Grut

LONDON AND NEW YORK

First published 2024
by Routledge
4 Park Square, Milton Park, Abingdon, Oxon OX14 4RN

and by Routledge
605 Third Avenue, New York, NY 10158

Routledge is an imprint of the Taylor & Francis Group, an informa business

English translation based on the Norwegian title *Digital kildekritikk* (ISBN 9788205529809), published with permission by Gyldendal, Oslo, Norway and translated to English by Diane Oatley. All figures are designed by Kristoffer Eidsnes.

British Library Cataloguing-in-Publication Data
A catalogue record for this book is available from the British Library

Library of Congress Cataloging-in-Publication Data
Names: Grut, Ståle, 1990– author.
Title: Evaluating digital sources in journalism : an introduction to digital source criticism / Ståle Grut.
Description: 1st. | London ; New York : Routledge, 2024. |
Series: Routledge focus on journalism studies |
Includes bibliographical references and index.
Identifiers: LCCN 2023044916 (print) | LCCN 2023044917 (ebook) |
ISBN 9781032590479 (hardback) | ISBN 9781032582948 (paperback) |
ISBN 9781003449461 (ebook)
Subjects: LCSH: Online journalism. | Attribution of news. |
Journalism–History–21st century.
Classification: LCC PN4784.O62 G78 2024 (print) |
LCC PN4784.O62 (ebook) | DDC 070.4–dc23/eng/20231016
LC record available at https://lccn.loc.gov/2023044916
LC ebook record available at https://lccn.loc.gov/2023044917

ISBN: 9781032590479 (hbk)
ISBN: 9781032582948 (pbk)
ISBN: 9781003449461 (ebk)

DOI: 10.4324/9781003449461

Typeset in Times New Roman
by Newgen Publishing UK

Contents

Preface

Source criticism is the process of evaluating a source, disclosing its tendency – or *bias* – and judging its credibility. The methodology of source criticism has roots in historical scholarship, and is often in English-speaking countries tied to the study of religious texts. In Scandinavia, the source-critical tradition is both long and strong. This critical approach to sources has today become part and parcel of journalistic practice in the region, and informs the practices of government, public education and beyond.

In the wake of the introduction of the Internet and new digital communication channels, the idea of a "digital source criticism" has been introduced. While sources can come in many forms, digital and online sources pose some new and unique challenges. Proper evaluation of digital and online sources requires new approaches, methods and tools. The aim of this book is to introduce timeless best practice and theoretical concepts in an accessible manner along with general advice on how to go about evaluating popular online sources.

The book summarises years of professional experience in the practice and study of journalism and digital culture. It collates a broad range of insights from professionals in the media industry, academia and the field of digital technology and communication. Much of the information presented in this book has primarily been shared in social media updates, blog posts, conference presentations and industry publications, but rarely gathered, contextualised and presented in an expository form. The goal of this book is to do just that and make that information accessible for students and others in need of an introduction to methods that are currently reshaping journalistic practice. The insights constitute a novel approach to breaking news, digital investigative journalism, online open-source investigations, advanced research or open-source intelligence (OSINT) – all of which rely on the practice of digital source criticism to varying degrees. Should you wish to explore in further depth the various topics and examples provided throughout, the book contains ample references to relevant source materials.

Originally published in Norwegian in 2021, this English edition contains some examples and literature from the Norwegian media landscape. These Norwegian examples have been selected due to their universality, their highlighting of central points of tension in the field of digital source criticism and their relevance to an international audience. Many novel and advanced approaches to source assessment and the evaluation of information are also included. Hopefully, this makes the book suitable for anyone wishing to advance their skills in assessing information – and especially for students in media and information literacy, journalism, media, communication, or library and information science.

Acknowledgements

The Fritt Ord Foundation helped fund this translation from Norwegian. The Fritt Ord Foundation, the Norwegian Non-Fiction Writers and Translators Association and Biblioteksvederlagsfondet – Pressens Faglitteraturfond all contributed to funding the original book.

Introduction

We currently have an abundance of digital sources at our fingertips, thanks to the Internet. The many devices we use on a daily basis provide a perpetual stream of notifications offering news, information and ads – all from various sources. Yet because our access to information has increased so dramatically, it has become more difficult to establish the accuracy and credibility of that information. The easy access to the web's abundance of information makes it all the more challenging to determine the original source and to establish the credibility of content.

To safely navigate the digital information landscape, we are dependent on applying and constantly updating our knowledge about *digital source criticism*. This is especially important for journalists, who carry out digital source criticism on behalf of their audience. Although new technical tools designed to assist in this endeavour are being introduced all the time, relying on such tools in isolation will never be a solution. In grappling with the challenges of digital content, our most important bulwark is a healthy scepticism combined with knowledge of the different methods and types of manipulation.

The book's structure

This book contains four chapters. Chapter 1 outlines the frameworks of traditional and a digital source criticism. The Scandinavian tradition of source criticism is presented, and the need for a new form of source criticism to address the challenges of digital content is established. This practice – digital source criticism – is illustrated through specific examples.

DOI: 10.4324/9781003449461-1

Chapter 2 addresses various forms of digital manipulation and illustrates why knowledge of digital source criticism is necessary for anybody using the Internet today. In the digital space, the manipulation of sources is widespread. This represents a great challenge for traditional source criticism as we know it. There are many different motives for manipulating digital content, and journalists must be aware of the risk of unknowingly spreading erroneous information to a large audience. The book elucidates methods of Internet and digital media content manipulation, as well as techniques for its identification and disclosure.

Chapter 3 demonstrates how journalists can uncover online content manipulation through a process of clarifying provenance and credibility, often referred to as *verification*. While the chapter predominantly addresses the verification of user-generated content (UGC) that is disseminated online and through social networks, several types of digital content and approaches to the latter are also discussed. The key here is to be able to verify the information you encounter online. The ability to analyse different types of statistics and numerical data is also central to digital source criticism, and the chapter delineates the rudimentary knowledge required for any journalist collating this type of information in news coverage.

The book's final chapter directs the source-critical lens outward and into the future, exploring how expertise in digital source criticism can lead to exciting revelations and new stories. Knowledge about how information is structured online, both by humans and machines, is essential for any journalist working with digital sources in our time. A number of actors, interest groups and media organisations have leveraged this knowledge, digging into the web's open sources in innovative ways in recent years. While multi-faceted, this work is often described using the military term OSINT (open-source intelligence). The chapter provides a core introduction to the art of investigating open sources in a journalistic context. A range of examples are provided to inspire journalists whether they are working alone or on staff in a newsroom.

1 Digital sources

A critical approach

Digital source criticism in four simple steps

We have never had as much information at our fingertips as we do at the present time, and with this availability comes the risk of undue influence. Digital propaganda and disinformation are designed to trick you into investing time and energy in the consumption of questionable content. For precisely this reason, you should be careful about where you focus your attention, because in our times it is one of the most valuable things you possess. This is best accomplished by practising digital source criticism when consuming information on and from the Internet.

A good place to start is with the four basic steps of the simple model for digital source criticism created by digital literacy expert Mike Caulfield.[1] The steps should be followed every time you experience strong reactions such as joy, anger or pride in response to something you come across online. For journalists, this reaction may take the form of a compulsion to share or write an article about something they have just seen or read. Instead of doing so, we should stop and reconsider. Any claims that trigger an emotional response should be subjected to diligent fact-checking.[2] In today's digital reality, we can set the bar even lower: we should investigate the facts behind every piece of information that captures our attention.[3] You should therefore make a habit of carrying out the following four steps every time you come across a statement or content that appears questionable:

1 Stop!

This is a relatively simple step and if you haven't yet acquired this classic critical reflex, then you should start developing it immediately.

DOI: 10.4324/9781003449461-2

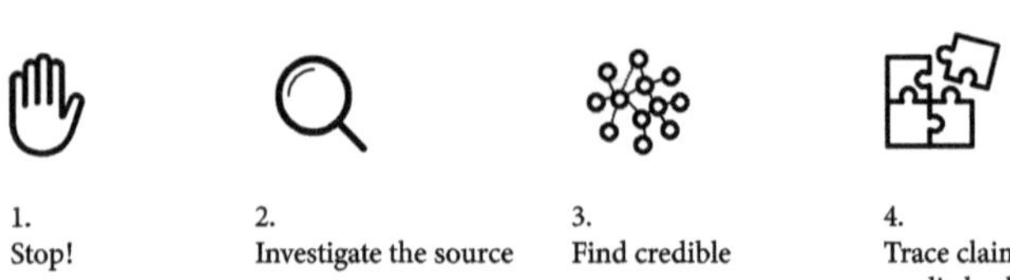

Figure 1.1 Mike Caulfield's SIFT-method illustrating four practical moves designed to reconstruct necessary context in order to effectively read, view or listen to digital content.

If you experience a strong emotional response, stop and ask yourself if you trust and are familiar with the source or information before you. Remember that even experienced and well-known journalists can be careless at this stage. If you detect any feelings of uncertainty, you should carry out the subsequent steps of the model. Do not give the content any further attention or share it with anyone else until you know what it is *actually* about and, if possible, who is responsible for the content. Develop the habit of stopping and thinking in this way.

2 Investigate the source

The point now is to ensure that you know *what* you are reading *before* you read it. This doesn't mean that you have to produce a detailed research report about absolutely everything you find online, but let's say that you read something about economics written by a reputable economist. It is then relevant to know why the author is considered reputable and by which interest groups in this particular field.[4] If you see a video on the benefits of oil and gas export, you should have knowledge about whether the video was produced or financed by an interest organisation within the oil and gas sector. The point is that reputable economists are not always right and neither are interest groups always wrong. What is important here is to gain knowledge of the source's expertise and what the source may be trying to achieve, so you can interpret their claims with this context in mind.

Spend 30 seconds searching for multiple trusted online sources that corroborate the source's credibility before you start to read. This will help you determine whether it makes sense to spend any more time reading the content in depth. The more frequently you do this, the more quickly you will complete the process the next time around.

3 Find credible coverage

It's not always the case that the content itself is what is of interest. Maybe you want to determine the accuracy of a claim in the intro or headline. Maybe the standpoint being presented is in fact universally accepted. Or maybe it is controversial.

In this particular case, the best strategy is to stop and ignore the source in front of you. Seek out credible journalism or research that will provide an independent analysis of the claim. Do an internet search for the best source that has covered this issue and, again, consult multiple sources. What is the consensus? Has in-depth, investigative journalism or fact-checking been carried out previously? In order to evaluate the credibility of any claim, it is important to understand its context and background.

4 Trace claims, quotes and media back to the original context

The first step in practising good digital source criticism often involves tracing claims, quotes and media back to the original source. Who said what and what did they *really* say? Only by getting to the bottom of this will you be able to assess the accuracy of subsequent renditions. You can read more about how to do this in Chapter 3.

A great deal of the information floating around on the Internet has been torn out of context. A common recurring example in news coverage is video footage of violence in connection with demonstrations. If you see such footage, you should consider the following: What happened before the clip began? Who caused the situation to escalate? What was edited out or concealed in the video and what was included? Perhaps the footage seems credible, but the description or title doesn't make sense. Does the video footage actually come from the situation in question? How did it end up on the Internet? Who is behind the user account that shared it? This applies not only to video footage but also to other types of illustrations, infographics, graphs and even maps. What is the source of the illustrations? How was the data compiled and presented? What research is the data based on? Are the illustrations actually misleading the reader? As a journalist, you should be able to answer these questions and preferably make it possible for the public to perform a simple check. You increase your credibility by showing your readers or viewers your cards, so it is a good habit to always include details and links to further information about the sources you have used.

The epistemic foundation of source criticism

For most people, the above four steps will be adequate. Nonetheless, it is useful for journalists to acquire in-depth knowledge about how digital source criticism is carried out and what it actually means. A natural starting point would be to develop an understanding of traditional source criticism. The word *source* is basically used in reference to information and assertions of relevance to a specific issue.[5] In principle, *anything* that can contribute to increasing our knowledge about the past or the present can be a source.[6] In journalism, oral sources are commonly used, as are written sources such as documents and journals.[7] Today, content from digital, web-based sources is a valuable resource in any journalist's daily life.

Professor Bente Kalsnes summarises source criticism as an epistemological approach that raises questions about how knowledge is obtained and how we can evaluate information sources.[8] While the concept has developed in various directions and different fields, central roots of source criticism can be traced back to the German historian Leopold von Ranke (1795–1886). Ranke has greatly influenced the development of historical scholarship, promoted rigorous fact-checking as a key to mastering the craft of historical research, and has been referred to as a "father of historical science".[9] According to Ranke, the historian should reconstruct the past as it actually was, per his dictum *wie es eigentlich gewesen ist*, and not impose one's own views and values.[10] A prerequisite for achieving this factually and impartially was by way of an objective scientific methodology, working with original sources and documents, rather than reproductions.[11] The idea that the best way to investigate any topic is to come as close to the original source as possible is also important when working in the digital space, where copies and modifications flourish. Ranke's critical approach to sources became a gold standard for historical research and writing during the nineteenth century, and as the field of history was professionalised, the methods reverberated throughout the world.[12] However, after the First World War, a shift in the historiographical focus sought to broaden the scope of Ranke's – sometimes misunderstood – exclusively fact-oriented approach to historical analysis, which resulted in a waning of its influence in English-speaking countries, according to historian George Iggers.[13] In Germany and Scandinavia, however, source criticism has been pivotal in historical research, and had broader societal impact, especially in government and education.[14]

A central source of inspiration for the modern practice of source criticism is the German philosopher Hans-Georg Gadamer, who considers truth to be inescapably connected to interpretation and understanding. In his seminal work *Truth and Method*, truth is posited as evolving, rooted in the interpretation and re-interpretation of the available sources of information.[15] Because journalism predominantly focuses on truth as related to social life, the binary epistemology that structures the traditional method of verification in journalism – true/false, fake/real – can fall short.[16] Instead, by following Gadamer's lead, truth becomes tied to an ongoing process of interpretation. Interpreting a phenomenon is guided by a level of understanding. This leads to novel interpretations and understandings, which can in turn guide interpretation. In short, understanding guides interpretation, and vice versa, in a potentially infinite cycle.[17] Since a video, an image, a document or an Instagram post – source materials –according to Gadamer will always be influenced by those sources' "horizon of understanding" – the origin, its broader sociocultural context, and factors such as language and genre – all sources and source material have bias, or in source-critical parlance: a *tendency*.[18] A key process in source-critical practice is to reveal such tendencies and their influence on the source material you are evaluating.

Journalism professor Steen Steensen et al. offer a pertinent example connecting the hermeneutical process outlined by Gadamer to journalism, as well as journalists' work with digital sources.[19] Imagine a journalist who is covering a claim made by a politician. The claim is put forth in a social media post. It contains a link and an image, purportedly supporting the claim. The journalist's prior knowledge – and natural understanding – of the politician (source) and social media post (source material) enacts a series of interpretations of the post, and subsequently the link. If the journalist recognises the URL, he or she repeats the same procedure, interpreting the latter source (URL) and source material (website) and how they relate to the politician's claim. The process then moves on to the image, the third form of source material, where the interpretation is based on prior knowledge of similar images, other references in visual culture the journalist knows of and so forth. The journalist's interpretations are coloured by prior knowledge about the topic in question, and its social, cultural, technological and political contexts – as well as other sources and source material consulted before beginning to produce the story. If the journalist encounters sources or source material that offer an entirely different perspective, this introduces a renewed interpretation of the post, the link, the image or all three of them. Following publication, input from readers and the public can lead to further understandings and interpretations. Even future source material, such as similar posts from other politicians, will engender new understandings and re-interpretation of the source material in this example.

Journalists have in common with historians, scientists and investigators that they must often reconstruct the past in different ways, in order to understand and explain an event or issue to their public. Source criticism explains how sources should be handled in order to prevent distortion of the information they provide.[20] In his introductory work to the field of history, Knut Kjeldstadli writes that if you are going to construct a building out of explanations, you need a foundation made of solid statements about something that did or did not happen – about *who* did *what*, *when* and *how*.[21] This foundation is made up of four "walls":

- *What are your sources?* The sources should be comprehensive or *representative*. For journalists, the latter specifically entails ensuring a balanced and diverse selection of sources that does not exclude a particular type of observation or insight.[22]
- *What types of sources are they?* Can you determine the origin and purpose of the source material and the source's function in the situation and environment in which it appeared? How *current* is the source material in relation to the subject under investigation?
- *What does the source say?* Your job as an investigator of a source is to interpret the contents of the source materials. Does the source demonstrate any *tendency (bias)* – intentions, interests or other considerations that could influence the interpretation of the source material?[23]
- *How will you use the source?* The source material has *relevance* for you as a journalist when it answers or contributes to answering the questions, theories and hypotheses you have about a subject.[24]

Source criticism for journalists

This foundation gives us a solid basis for exploring in further depth source criticism's role in journalism. Below follows a review of some key terms found in source-critical practice in journalism, corresponding with the four walls described above, specifically: representativity, currency, bias and relevance.

Representativity: You ensure the representativity of your sources by providing a satisfactory selection of all possible sources, so the issue in question is illuminated from a range of perspectives and without excluding a specific type of observation.[25] A journalist cannot compete with researchers or polling agencies when it comes to acquiring a representative selection. In purely practical terms, a *reasonable range* should therefore be the objective for every journalist endeavouring to ensure representativity. Keeping this within the realm of feasibility in a practical sense would imply that the selection of sources cannot be too broad; but with an eye to achieving an acceptable level of valid relevance, neither can the selection be too small.[26]

Single-source journalism is not uncommon in the news media and often appears in the form of recurring digital stories – short articles based on another media story or a report from a news agency.[27] The opposite of the one-source story is investigative journalism, in which the journalist does not solely refer to what has happened and who has said what, but also works with an eye to uncovering facts that reveal discrepancies.[28]

Currency: It is often necessary to make an assessment of the amount of time that has passed between a source's observation and the account of the observed events, and whether there have been other parties involved in the final account. This helps to clarify the type of source you have before you. In a canonised work on source criticism for journalism students, Egil Fossum and Sidsel Meyer summarise research on currency by saying that the greater the amount time that has passed since the occurrence of an event, the more caution we must exercise about trusting what has been said about it.[29] In the digital world, it is easy to manipulate temporal data, so you should be especially attentive to this. We will return to this in Chapter 2.

For journalists, it is also necessary to be able to distinguish between sources in time and space. First-hand sources, such as witnesses, have the closest connection to an event. If you have access to a first-hand source, this is your *primary source*, which is the most preferable type of source, because it is closest in time and space to the event in question.[30] Sources that do not share this proximity are *secondary sources*. What distinguishes second-hand sources from first-hand sources is that the former are based on a retelling or interpretation of others' experiences and accounts.[31] An example here would be a news story that discusses an eyewitness account, or encyclopaedia articles that are compilations of information from a variety of first-hand sources. If you only have access to second-hand sources for a story, these become your *primary sources*. The terms third-hand (or tertiary) and fourth-hand sources are also used and correspond with the degree of removal from a first-hand source. An example of a third-hand source would be a Wikipedia article, which will often cite second-hand sources such as news articles. Although it cites sources far afield from first-hand sources, Wikipedia remains a popular source, not least for the news media. With this in mind, Chapter 2 addresses how journalists can best employ Wikipedia.

Bias: Is there anything about the source's background, value base and intention that might introduce bias into the source material? Fossum and Meyer write that bias often complicates the relation between the information and the reality being addressed by that information. According to professor of media studies Sigurd Allern, varying degrees of bias or distortion are found in all sources. Allern nonetheless concludes that few partisan sources of today, such as politicians, CEOs, organisation members, activists or analysts, will benefit from promoting a false image of reality.[32] It is therefore up to the journalist to make an assessment of the source's bias. This must be done while keeping in mind that finding content wholly without any bias whatsoever is impossible.[33]

On behalf of the public, the journalist must therefore identify any interests that may be influencing the source material's underlying tendencies, so as to assess credibility, and potentially find more sources.[34] Allern writes that distinguishing between different types of statements is a useful starting point. A source that makes a statement about the facts of a matter (regarding a political interview, official statistics or surveys) will typically offer empirical claims which can be easily verified through other sources.[35] Bias comes into play when those who interpret or evaluate factual materials bring their values and the traditions of their discipline to bear in their assessments. This must be taken into account in the journalist's critical assessment of sources.

Relevance: For a journalist, a preliminary step in the work on any story is usually to acquire an overview of the sources of relevance to the story.[36] As stated above, source material has relevance for a journalist when it contributes to confirming or disproving a journalist's hypotheses and theories and answering a journalist's questions about a story.[37] A source can, to varying degrees, help with this task. You can save time on this step by reading summaries and key phrases before reading articles in their entirety. There are different degrees of relevance, and after having thoroughly investigated a source, it is not unlikely that you will end up discarding it because it does not have sufficient relevance to your story.

Traditional source criticism: a waste of time

Now that we have summarised the fundamental features of source criticism for journalists, it is also useful to look at the kind of source criticism typically used by and taught to the general public. This can provide a better understanding of the general public's source-critical abilities. The multitude of sources we have at our fingertips today makes it more difficult to navigate the available information. We are therefore dependent on having effective methods to do so. This is where source criticism comes in, or the criteria used to determine the type of information that does and does not merit our attention. Traditionally, when recommending the evaluation of a source, it is helpful to ask four general questions:[38]

- *Credibility*: Can you trust the source?
- *Objectivity*: Is the source neutral?
- *Accuracy*: Are there signs of disinformation or sloppiness?
- *Suitability*: Does the source provide the answers you need?

These are relevant and timeless questions to ask about written sources. To answer the questions, one is usually advised to investigate a source carefully to determine precisely what it contains and who has written it. Advice of this nature is often compiled in the form of a checklist that can be applied to different sources. With time, as sources have become digital and web-based, questions about website design and the functionality of links have been included on such checklists. The CRAAP test, a checklist used a great deal in the USA, is made up of 25 questions that you can ask when investigating a source. About internet sources, the list states that they are to be assessed on the basis of whether the links function and whether top-level domains such as .com or .org disclose information about the source.[39] Sites developed by renowned universities give similar advice about top-level domains and use of logos.[40] Lists of this nature contain clearly relevant questions to be asked about sources, but in a digital world the use of these lists alone will seldom be sufficient. The challenge we meet with almost immediately is that the digital world upends fundamental aspects of how we have traditionally carried out source criticism.

The control questions mentioned above can easily lead to erroneous conclusions. A website with an .org domain is not necessarily more credible than a site with a domain ending with .com. A convincing website with working links, credible logos and a professional layout can be created free of charge or purchased inexpensively. A website that appears to be local can in fact be run by unknown actors in another country. Such connections can prove difficult to disclose. Incorrect or misleading information can be easily presented in a credible framework on the Internet. It is just a matter of time before it will be possible to digitally mass-produce apparently credible – but fictitious – text, video content and other digital experiences which will further challenge our abilities to critically assess sources.[41]

This evolution requires us to establish a designated digital source criticism which takes into account the unique features of the Internet. A website is fundamentally different from a book or other printed materials, because it can be so easily and quickly changed and manipulated. A key aspect of digital source criticism is that it employs the features of entire networks to determine the degree of a source's credibility. The source is, after all, one node – a single point in a network made up of many points – so what can we actually learn about it from the rest of the network?

In a digital world fraught with lies and propaganda, we are obliged to be smarter than the classical source-criticism methods. If you sit down to read lies and propaganda and spend an enormous amount of time studying the author, the design and claims as a means of establishing credibility, you can quickly lose your way. Inducing the reader to become absorbed with propaganda rather than more neutral sources is precisely one of the intentions of creating and spreading propaganda. The time you could have spent on a reliable source is time you will never get back. As stated, with so many available sources, your attention is one of your most valuable assets in the digital age.[42] You should therefore be extremely careful about where you direct that attention.

The necessity of a digital source criticism

Through the concept of *digital methods*, Professor Richard A. Rogers makes the argument for a new approach to the Internet in research. Although classical academic methods such as surveys can be carried out digitally, Rogers highlights the need to adopt "the medium's methods" in order to investigate "natively digital objects".[43] Rogers cites web scraping, crowdsourcing and folksonomy as examples of wholly digital web techniques for the retrieval and sorting of data. Using digital methods, it is possible to investigate how these objects are treated by digital platforms and services such as Facebook and Google. One example would be algorithms, such as Google's PageRank, that are used to organise, rank and present information on the Internet. We must understand and learn how digital media handle links, hits, likes, tags, time stamps and other digitally created or real-life objects, if we are to research and investigate the Internet and the content derived through it. Rogers' goal is a new research practice that can ground claims relating to cultural change or societal conditions in online dynamics.[44] Naturally, it is also important to understand these digital systems and objects in order to carry out digital source criticism. By observing the development of web services and digital media, the objective of Rogers' digital methods is to adapt in step with this development. Because the Internet is both so accessible and so easily exploited, digital methods open the door for combining digital objects in new ways.[45] A best practice in digital source criticism considers the unique challenges (and possibilities) of digital media, and how a source-critical approach can contribute to obtaining more information about a digital object. It recognises a platform's impact on the content within it. It also recognises the need for checking multiple sources and that acquiring greater understanding of digital networks and services is critical to the process of digital source criticism. The latter is ever evolving in step with technological advances, and for a journalist, this would mean that the practice will often require interdisciplinary input from computer scientists, archivists, specialists and other journalists.

In a classic essay from 1985, Professor James Moor defined the field of *digital ethics*. Moor described how computers basically and at all times perform tasks behind the scenes, and thereby have invisible modes of operation that are difficult to grasp.[46] Moor states in the essay that "One may be quite knowledgeable about the inputs and outputs of a computer and only dimly aware of the internal processing". New technology is not a neutral tool. This currently finds expression in algorithms that trade in both discrimination and favouritism.[47] The Dutch editor Rob Wijnberg writes that today the algorithms have *become* the source.[48] The algorithms – the functioning and underlying criteria of which are heavily guarded trade secrets shrouded in mystery – have a huge influence on our worldview. Wijnberg writes that algorithms to a large extent determine the information and news that is created, how it is distributed and, ultimately, what the public is allowed to see. The algorithms thereby play a part in determining what we believe, think and know.

A clear bridge to source criticism becomes evident here, as well as why it must also include the digital aspect in order to evolve. Traditional source criticism has not had a compelling need or tradition for critical investigation of the medium in and of itself. Fossum and Meyer state in their textbook on source criticism in journalism that "What is written, is written. There is something permanent and unchanging about it. The die is cast".[49] They do add that the Internet and electronic publishing have altered this somewhat. Still, one of the reasons for writing the book you are reading right now is the extent to which the Internet and the digital world have changed the requirements for how we must relate to sources. The facility of digital alteration represents a clear challenge for journalists because source materials can be abruptly changed. The history of the web is being established as a separate field of research and study, but it is a field replete with challenges.[50] As a journalist you will often be obliged to rely on archived versions of a web-based source, with all the additional assessments this entails in terms of source criticism – if you are fortunate enough to find an existing archived version. Not everything on the Internet is saved, but institutions such as Internet Archive, a plethora of national libraries and others are nonetheless working to document parts of the Internet for posterity. Many researchers and institutions, especially in fields such as journalism, history and information studies, must grapple with digital sources and digital source materials today. Places where knowledge about this is being developed include the Roy Rosenzweig Center for History and New Media in Virginia, where digital solutions for source management have been developed that everyone can use, such as the reference tool Zotero and the photo management tool Tropy; and the Digital Methods Initiative at the University of Amsterdam, which offers a range of tools and courses for doing digital research.

Traditionally speaking, a requirement for performing source criticism is that you must have knowledge about your subject matter in order to approach sources – individuals and information – on a more or less equal footing.[51] Technology has not yet affected this requirement to any noteworthy extent, but the Internet alters a fundamental dimension of the information we engage with today: the arena in which one meets with sources. Technology also affects our encounters with sources in ways we don't notice. In the same way that one was required to know something about how society functioned in order to be a good journalist in an analogue era, you must possess a certain level of knowledge about how the Internet and digital services function to be a good journalist in a digital age.

To become truly digital, source criticism must therefore to a greater extent include the critical investigation of media in and of themselves, not solely the contents. In the digital sphere, there are many aspects of relevance to source criticism that are not covered by traditional methods. Much of this entails technical details such as algorithms. Ultimately, algorithms are the outcome of decisions made by human beings. The disclosure of connections and networks on the Internet as part of a source-critical analysis might seem straightforward in some cases. Yet it is potentially impossible at a time when the world's largest companies operate digital platforms and are often notoriously non-transparent in terms of how they make decisions and manage content.

Given the nature of the Internet's evolution, my position is that we should be fundamentally sceptical about everything we read there. Journalists should always carry out digital source criticism as a part of their work process. It is not difficult to find sensational content on the Internet, but if you cannot establish the origin, when the content arose and where it came from, the content should be neither used nor reproduced. Unfortunately, this fundamental insight is frequently ignored. Journalist Adi Robertson describes news in the age of the Internet as a version of the telephone game.[52] Instead of going directly to the source, different media outlets cite one another. This is easier and quicker but frequently leads to misunderstandings and the disappearance of important details every time a story is retold.

I experienced this first-hand after introducing a compulsory quiz for technology news articles published by the Norwegian Broadcasting Corporation (NRK). The feature, called "Know2Comment", requires the reader to answer three questions about an article before they are permitted to publish a comment. The feature was first noticed by Nieman Journalism Lab at Harvard, who interviewed us and wrote an in-depth article about the quiz.[53] Their article was subsequently picked up and quoted by international media outlets such as CNN, BBC and France 24. Naturally, many journalists all over the world read those stories. Amidst the hundreds of subsequent news reports that were produced about the quiz, a game of telephone commenced. Some reporters contacted us to request interviews of their own. Others cited the original interview done by Nieman Journalism Lab. Some quoted others' reproductions of this original interview, and added their own descriptions and observations, which were in turn picked up by other media. Key details from the original story receded further and further into the background with each subsequent reproduction.

Another relevant variant of this phenomenon occurred when the UK newspaper *The Telegraph* printed an article about billionaire Bill Gates' purchase of a brand-new luxury hydrogen-powered yacht.[54] The sensational story was reported by a huge number of news outlets globally. While most of the coverage cited *The Telegraph*, these stories rarely made reference to key details, such as the fact that the information in the original story came from an anonymous source. When the BBC's Zoe Kleinman later contacted the company responsible for building the yacht to do an interview, Kleinman was told that she was the first journalist to have been in touch with them. Kleinman also learned some critical information. Bill Gates had never bought the yacht. The story had travelled around the world, even though it was incorrect, because not a single journalist had gone to the trouble of contacting the most important source to corroborate the facts of the story.[55]

The effectiveness of network reading

Leveraging the inherent power of the Internet is a recurring theme in digital source criticism. An experiment done at Stanford University observed the approaches of historians, students and fact-checkers when addressing information on the Internet. The results revealed large differences in the approaches of these groups. The historians and students were fooled by easily manipulated features on the website, such as the domain name and logos that looked official.[56] The problem was that they read *vertically*. They remained on the website and studied it in depth to determine its credibility. This is exactly what a traditional checklist for source criticism will instruct you to do in meeting with a digital/online source. You perform a thorough investigation of the source itself, paradoxically to assess the credibility of the same source.

The fact-checkers who were observed used an approach diametrically opposed to that of the historians and students. They read *horizontally*. They quickly scanned the website and then instantly opened new tabs to check what other websites could tell them about the source and the information they were supposed to evaluate. Compared to the historians and students, the fact-checkers used a fraction of the time to establish whether or not they could vouch for the source. I call this technique *network reading*, precisely because in order to effectively evaluate the credibility of a digital source, we must read and interpret the surrounding network. The technique is also referred to as lateral reading or horizontal reading. The researchers responsible for the above study state that it is virtually pointless to spend 15 minutes on an internet article using a traditional checklist for source criticism, when you can consult Wikipedia and determine in a few seconds that what you are reading is actually an almost 30-year-old internet hoax that has long since been debunked.[57]

Most people will quickly understand that state-controlled media are not the best source of information about the degree of injustice and corruption on the part of the same country's authorities.[58] You can easily discover this through network reading. Good digital source criticism thereby becomes a series of digital habits – rules of thumb – which quickly disclose essential information, such as that a particular media platform is a part of a government's propaganda machine, or that an apparently lucrative financial product is actually a scam.

When you carry out traditional source criticism on digital media you may quickly find yourself in a challenging situation. Even though you can answer all the questions of relevance for an analogue checklist – such as identifying the author and the type of text – you are not necessarily on the right track. Often the most critical information is lacking, especially when it comes to understanding internet content: the context. Elements such as the use of symbols and choice of publication date or platform can seem innocent in and of themselves but may be motivated by the source's agenda. Awareness of this is important. Both the form and content will be relevant aspects of the context you must evaluate. Searching the outside network through network reading, to see what *other* nodes on the Internet have to say about the source node you are evaluating and other relevant information, is therefore key with an eye to saving time and disclosing the influence of sources that intentionally or unintentionally disseminate unreliable information.

Understanding the Internet's signals

We human beings often use heuristics when making decisions in daily life and naturally also when we are browsing the Internet. Simple rules like this are often helpful when it comes to drawing correct conclusions quickly but do not in fact guarantee the accuracy of these conclusions. The challenge in this context is that the heuristics we use to navigate in the real world are, at best, not relevant for, and at worst, easily confounded by a digital format.[59] Falsifying a public uprising on the streets is difficult, but followers and the affiliated "likes" on the Internet can be purchased on the cheap. Websites and platforms can also be manipulated to agitate for one actor's view. Identifying information that can and *cannot* be trusted on the Internet is a uniquely digital challenge, and one which former teachings about source criticism do not adequately equip us to address.[60]

Even though some user accounts on social media have an official "verified" symbol beside their name, this does not mean that they disseminate verified information. Although information is found on the Internet, this does not automatically mean that it is credible. There is a long list of techniques for manipulating content on the Internet and social media. A wrench in this particular machinery is the fact that it is more difficult to simulate a long history and broad internet presence for a user account than to make an account appear popular at the current time. It is difficult, if not impossible, to backdate a publication on social networking sites. That is one of the reasons why older and established user accounts that over an extended time period have produced somewhat credible content can be sold at a higher price as followers than user accounts that have been only registered recently.[61] If a source registered a user account several years ago and consequently has had a consistent and long-term online presence, this is a factor that suggests credibility. Because followers, likes, shares and other social network interactions can be easily bought and sold, making a user account appear popular here and now is a cinch. A user account with several million followers that was registered a week ago is therefore not necessarily more credible than a user account with only a thousand followers that was registered ten years ago.

An incident from London serves as good example of how seemingly credible internet content can actually be a fabrication. *VICE* magazine writer Oobah Butler registered a new restaurant there on the website Tripadvisor. What was unique about this restaurant was that it did not exist. On the basis of fictive reviews, the non-existent restaurant was eventually ranked number one among more than 18,000 restaurants in London. Requests poured in for reservations from all over the world. Butler's friends and family had been hired to write fictional reviews and were instructed to give *consistent* descriptions of the menu, of how difficult it was to get a table and how the restaurant visit itself had been a strange experience.[62] The reviews were published from different digital devices to ensure that the ruse would not be detected. This relatively simple manipulation succeeded in fooling one of the largest travel websites in the world, a website which in its own advertising boasts of its use of advanced technology to weed out false reviews, into presenting a fictional restaurant as the absolute best eatery in London.

Such examples are comparable to the strategies of social platforms such as Facebook and YouTube with regard to how they prioritise content that generates user engagement. This in turn influences the type of content that appears on the social media sites to different users, without there being any simple explanation or visible mechanisms to explain why this occurs. Factor in that the platforms' underlying algorithms are, as stated above, notoriously non-transparent and considered trade secrets. The manipulation of these platforms can have ripple effects in society. Content that erroneously appears to be popular on the Internet can receive a disproportionate amount of attention or gain a position of prominence on the public agenda on the basis of the *perception* of popularity.

The media have an essential role to play here. In the absence of digital source criticism, the media will help strengthen the impact of these platforms on society, by devoting editorial attention to information on an unfounded basis.[63] Unlike journalism, the platforms take little or no responsibility for the veracity of published content, and this is something every journalist must keep in mind when approaching these sources. Facebook states clearly that "We don't have a policy that stipulates that the information you post on Facebook must be true".[64] Social media users can personally edit usernames, biographies and contact info at any time. The platforms highlight their own preferred metrics, such as number of followers, comments, likes and active users within a favourable time frame. The various platforms also operate with different and often non-transparent requirements for what constitutes a share or a view. As a journalist you should therefore be able to carry out investigations that look beyond these metrics to disclose critical facts about a user account, a network of user accounts or an apparently popular video or other content.

For any journalist, writing a story about a claim that "makes the Internet explode" is a simple matter. However, it is more challenging and resource-intensive to assess the basis for such claims. Due to the way the platforms present data, it is almost impossible to ascertain how many of perhaps hundreds of thousands of shares are done by actual human beings. What we do know with certainty is that a large number of posts and a large amount of the activity on social media are created by user accounts of unknown origins. It is therefore a paradox that figures indicating high share, play and view counts on social media remain a constant topic of headlines in the news media.

Questions for reflection and exercises

- Think of a few sources you consult for information on a daily basis. These might include Google Search, Google News, YouTube, Instagram or WhatsApp. Do you know how these services select their information? Is it possible to find out?
- Look at somebody else's version of a service or app that you use such as Facebook. How different is your experience of these services and apps from the experiences of others?
- Read Rob Wijnberg's essay about algorithms in *The Correspondent*, entitled "How the Truth Became Whatever Makes You Click". The link is included in the reference list. Do you agree with the claims made in the essay?
- Surf a bit on the Internet and select a sensational news item. Then apply the four steps described at the beginning of this chapter to the story. The steps are 1) stop, 2) investigate the source, 3) find credible coverage and 4) trace claims, quotes and media back to the original context. What did you learn?
- Do an inventory of the sources you have been in contact with recently. How many of these were analogue? How many were

digital? Think about how frequently you go to the original sources of articles you read in online newspapers or elsewhere on the Internet.

Notes

1 Mike Caulfield, *Introducing SIFT, a Four Moves Acronym* (12 May 2019). Accessed 1 November 2019. Available at Hapgood hapgood.us/2019/05/12/sift-and-a-check-please-preview
2 Mike Caulfield, Chapter 3: Building a Fact-Checking Habit by Checking Your Emotions in *Web Literacy for Student Fact-Checkers* (8 January 2017). Accessed 6 September 2019. Available at Pressbooks webliteracy.pressbooks.com/chapter/building-a-habit-by-checking-your-emotions
3 Adi Robertson, *How to fight lies, tricks, and chaos online* (3 December 2019). Accessed 5 December 2019. Available at The Verge theverge.com/2019/12/3/20980741/fake-news-facebook-twitter-misinformation-lies-fact-check-how-to-internet-guide
4 Mike Caulfield, Introducing SIFT in *Check, Please! Starter Course* (2019). Accessed 12 September 2019. Available at Notion notion.so/04db7879dd7a4efaa76bfb2397d11ffd
5 Sigurd Allern & Ester Pollack, *Källkritik! – Journalistik i lögnens tid [Source criticism! – Journalism in the Age of Lies]* (2019). Studentlitteratur AB, p. 69.
6 Ibid, p. 71.
7 Egil Fossum & Sidsel Meyer, *Er nå det så sikkert? [How can you be so sure?]* (2008). Cappelen Damm Akademisk, p. 128.
8 Bente Kalsnes, *Introducing Digital Source Criticism: A Method for Tackling Fake News and Disinformation.* In Stefania M. Maci, Massimiliano Demata, Mark McGlashan, & Philip Seargeant (Eds.), *Routledge Handbook of Discourse and Disinformation* (2023). Routledge.
9 George G. Iggers, *Introduction.* In Leopold von Ranke, *The Theory and Practice of History* (2010) Routledge.
Andreas Fickers, Stefania Scagliola, and Andy O'Dwyer, *Exploring the origin and use of the term "digital source criticism"* (2017). Accessed 28. August 2023. Available at Ranke.2 ranke2.uni.lu/de/define-dsc/skilltraining.html
10 Knut Kjeldstadli, *Fortida er ikke hva den en gang var [The past isn't what it once was]* (2007). Universitetsforlaget, p. 169.
George G. Iggers, *Introduction.* In Leopold von Ranke, *The Theory and Practice of History* (2010). Routledge.
11 Knut Kjeldstadli, *Fortida er ikke hva den en gang var [The past isn't what it once was]* (2007). Universitetsforlaget.

12 George G. Iggers, *Introduction*. In Leopold von Ranke, *The Theory and Practice of History* (2010). Routledge.
13 Ibid.
14 Peter Edelberg & Dorthe Gert Simonsen, *Changing the Subject: Epistemologies of Scandinavian source criticism* (2015) Scandinavian Journal of History, *40*, 215–238. doi.org/10.1080/03468755.2015.1021276 Fredrik Bertilsson, *Source Criticism as a Technology of Government in the Swedish Psychological Defence: The Impact of Humanistic Knowledge on Contemporary Security Policy* (2021) Humanities, 10(1), doi.org/10.3390/h10010013
15 Steen Steensen et al, *Journalism and Source Criticism. Revised Approaches to Assessing Truth-Claims* (2022). Journalism Studies, 0(0), 1–19. doi.org/10.1080/1461670X.2022.2140446
16 Ibid.
17 Ibid.
18 Hans-Georg Gadamer, *Truth and Method* (2013) London: Bloomsbury Academic as cited in Steen Steensen et al, *Journalism and Source Criticism. Revised Approaches to Assessing Truth-Claims* (2022). Journalism Studies, 0(0), 1–19. doi.org/10.1080/1461670X.2022.2140446
19 Ibid.
20 Knut Kjeldstadli, *Fortida er ikke hva den en gang var [The past isn't what it once was]* (2007). Universitetsforlaget, p. 169.
21 Ibid.
22 Egil Fossum & Sidsel Meyer, *Er nå det så sikkert? [How can you be so sure?]* (2008). Cappelen Damm Akademisk, p. 61.
23 Ibid, p. 75.
24 Ibid, p. 59.
25 Ibid, p. 60.
26 Ibid, p. 61.
27 Sigurd Allern, *Journalistikk og kildekritisk analyse [Journalism and source critical analysis]* (2015). Cappelen Damm Akademisk, p. 40.
28 Rune Ytreberg in Morten Møller Warmedal & Guri Hjeltnes, *Gravende journalistikk [Investigative journalism]* (2012). Gyldendal Akademisk, p. 146.
29 Egil Fossum & Sidsel Meyer, *Er nå det så sikkert? [How can you be so sure?]* (2008). Cappelen Damm Akademisk, p. 77.
30 Knut Kjeldstadli, *Fortida er ikke hva den en gang var [The past isn't what it once was]* (2007). Universitetsforlaget, p. 177.
31 Sigurd Allern, *Journalistikk og kildekritisk analyse [Journalism and source critical analysis]* (2015). Cappelen Damm Akademisk, p. 38.
32 Ibid, p. 50.
33 Egil Fossum & Sidsel Meyer, *Er nå det så sikkert? [How can you be so sure?]* (2008). Cappelen Damm Akademisk, p. 75.
34 Ibid.

35 Sigurd Allern, *Journalistikk og kildekritisk analyse [Journalism and source critical analysis]* (2015). Cappelen Damm Akademisk, p. 51.

36 Ibid, p. 39.

37 Egil Fossum & Sidsel Meyer, *Er nå det så sikkert? [How can you be so sure?]* (2008). Cappelen Damm, p. 59.

38 Kristin Skare Orgeret, *kildekritikk [source criticism]* (13 December 2018). Accessed 4 September 2019. Available at Store norske leksikon snl.no/kildekritikk

39 Meriam Library at California State University, *Evaluating Information – Applying the CRAAP Test* (PDF dated 17 September 2010). Accessed 25 October 2019. Available at Meriam Library. Library.csuchico.edu/sites/default/files/craap-test.pdf

40 *Kildekompasset [The source compass]*, a guideline created by the University College of South-Eastern Norway, University of Agder and University of Stavanger (last updated 11 May 2015). Accessed 5 November 2019. Available at Kildekompasset kildekompasset.no/kildekritikk/nettsider/spraak-og-layout.aspx

Search & Write [Søk & Skriv], *Nettsider [Websites]* (15 November 2018). Accessed 7 April 2020. Available at Søk & Skriv sokogskriv.no/kildebruk-og-referanser/kildevurdering/kvalitative-vurderinger/nettadresser-url Archived version: web.archive.org/web/20181107032747/https://sokogskriv.no/kildebruk-og-referanser/kildevurdering/kvalitative-vurderinger/nettadresser-url

41 Examples are Google or OpenAI's language models, which can write text on the basis of a few key words. This is explained in further detail by Henrik Lied in *Noen tastetrykk er nok til å masseprodusere falske nyheter [A few keystrokes are enough to mass-produce fake news]* (7 November 2019). Accessed 18 December 2019. Available at NRKbeta nrkbeta.no/2019/11/07/noen-tastetrykk-er-nok-til-a-masseprodusere-falske-nyheter

For an example of such videos see Destin Sandlin, *Manipulating the YouTube Algorithm – (Part 1/3) Smarter Every Day 213* (31 March 2019). Accessed 18 December 2019. Available on YouTube youtu.be/1PGm8LslEb4

42 Claudio Celis Bueno, *The Attention Economy: Labour, Time and Power in Cognitive Capitalism* (2016). Rowman & Littlefield Publishers, p. 3.

43 Richard Rogers, *Digital Methods* (2013). MIT Press, p. 1.

44 Richard Rogers, *The end of the virtual: Digital methods* (2009). Inaugural lecture; No. 339. Vossiuspers UvA.

45 Richard Rogers, *Digital Methods* (2013). MIT Press, p. 1.

46 James H. Moor, *What Is Computer Ethics?* In Metaphilosophy, 16(4), 266–275 (1985). Accessed 8 April 2020. Available at Wiley Online Library doi.org/10.1111/j.1467-9973.1985.tb00173.x

47 Leonora Onarheim Bergsjø & Håkon Bergsjø, *Digital etikk [Digital ethics]* (2019). Universitetsforlaget, p. 15.
48 Rob Wijnberg, *How the truth became whatever makes you click* (16 April 2020). Accessed 16 April 2020. Available at The Correspondent thecorrespondent.com/410/how-the-truth-became-whatever-makes-you-click/5780615830-34c40db4
49 Egil Fossum & Sidsel Meyer, *Er nå det så sikkert? [How can you be so sure?]* (2008). Cappelen Damm.
50 Niels Brügger, *Website history and the website as an object of study* (2009). New Media & Society, 11(1–2), 115–132 doi.org/10.1177/1461444808099574
51 Sigurd Allern, *Journalistikk og kildekritisk analyse [Journalism and source critical analysis]* (2015). Cappelen Damm Akademisk, pp. 51–52.
52 Adi Robertson, *How to fight lies, tricks, and chaos online* (3 December 2019). Accessed 5 December 2019. Available at The Verge theverge.com/2019/12/3/20980741/fake-news-facebook-twitter-misinformation-lies-fact-check-how-to-internet-guide
53 Joseph Lichterman, *This site is "taking the edge off rant mode" by making readers pass a quiz before commenting* (1 March 2017). Accessed 23 October 2023. Available at Nieman Lab www.niemanlab.org/2017/03/this-site-is-taking-the-edge-off-rant-mode-by-making-readers-pass-a-quiz-before-commenting/
54 Zoe Kleinman, *Bill Gates "not buying our hydrogen yacht*" (10 February 2020). Accessed 16 April 2020. Available at BBC News bbc.com/news/technology-51446663
55 Zoe Kleinman, "*The yacht designer firm said I am the only journalist who has contacted them to ask whether this viral story was true*." (10 February 2020). Accessed 16 April 2020. Available at Twitter twitter.com/zsk/status/1226857259747151883
56 Sam Wineburg & Sarah McGrew, *Lateral Reading: Reading Less and Learning More When Evaluating Digital Information* (6 October 2017). Accessed 6 September 2019. Available at Social Science Research Network papers.ssrn.com/abstract=3048994
57 Sarah McGrew, Teresa Ortega, Joel Breakstone & Sam Wineburg, *The Challenge That's Bigger than Fake News: Civic Reasoning in a Social Media Environment* (2017). Accessed 5 September 2019. Available at American Educator, 41(3), 4 eric.ed.gov/?id=EJ1156387
58 John Warner, *Getting Beyond the CRAAP Test: A Conversation with Mike Caulfield* (14 august 2019). Accessed 3 September 2019. Available at Inside Higher Ed insidehighered.com/blogs/just-visiting/getting-beyond-craap-test-conversation-mike-caulfield

59 Mike Caulfield, *Network Heuristics* (28 March 2019). Accessed 3 September 2019. Available at Hapgood hapgood.us/2019/03/28/network-heuristics

60 Mike Caulfield writes in the previously mentioned "*Network Heuristics*": "[…] knowing what is trustworthy as a sign on the web and what is not is, unfortunately, uniquely digital knowledge."

61 Rory Smith & Carlotta Dotto, *The not-so-simple science of social media 'bots'* (28 November 2019). Accessed 5 December 2019. Available at First Draft firstdraftnews.org/latest/the-not-so-simple-science-of-social-media-bots

62 Ståle Grut, *Oobah Butler bruker nettet for å tukle med virkeligheten [Oobah Butler uses the internet to tinker with reality]* (3 June 2019). Accessed 12 January 2020. Available at NRKbeta nrkbeta.no/2019/06/03/oobah-butler-bruker-nettet-for-a-tukle-med-virkeligheten

63 Logan Molyneux & Shannon McGregor, *Think twice before turning to Twitter* (31 December 2019). Accessed 12 January 2020. Available at Nieman Lab niemanlab.org/2019/12/think-twice-before-turning-to-twitter

64 Drew Harwell, *Facebook acknowledges Pelosi video is faked but declines to delete it* (24 May 2019). Accessed 3 September 2019. Available at The Washington Post washingtonpost.com/technology/2019/05/24/facebook-acknowledges-pelosi-video-is-faked-declines-delete-it

2 Digital manipulation and disinformation

Introduction

The Internet offers an abundance of fascinating, credible and often high-quality information. Unfortunately, to an increasing extent this information is rivalled by manipulated and false content. It is therefore a good idea to be aware of a number of pitfalls. For journalists who will be evaluating sources on behalf of readers and viewers, it is important to understand the underlying motivation for and the techniques employed in the manipulation of media content, in order to be equipped to identify this.

Figures from Facebook and Twitter show that a large number of user accounts on these platforms are what they call fake accounts. In this book, the term "fake" is predominantly used in reference to information and user accounts claiming to be something or someone other than they actually are. For years, Facebook and Twitter have consistently estimated that around 5 per cent of all user accounts on their platforms are fake. If we base our assessment on Ipsos' estimates for Norwegian user accounts, there are close to 3.4 million Facebook users in Norway.[1] Given Facebook's claim that at least 5 per cent of user accounts are fake, this means that there can be more than 150,000 fake Facebook accounts in Norway alone. In addition to this, Facebook estimates that 11 per cent of user accounts are what they call duplicates, in other words, accounts actually administrated by a person who already has a Facebook account.[2]

Many of the fundamental building blocks for the Internet were developed half a century ago. Internet security lay in the fact that the Internet was made up of distributed systems connected through a network, which meant that the systems would continue to function even if

DOI: 10.4324/9781003449461-3

parts of that network were disabled. Fundamental security mechanisms for communication, such as encryption, were not introduced until later on. It is therefore possible to manipulate elements of the Internet's basic functionality, a possibility that is exploited through hacker attacks on e-mail accounts and other digital infrastructure. Because of this, services such as e-mail, the worldwide web and SMS are at their core vulnerable to manipulation, even today. More recent apps and services have often activated powerful encryption across multiple layers, but in many cases, it is still possible to send a fictional e-mail or SMS from what appears to be a genuine source. Content such as images and videos can be altered and generated using powerful and increasingly available software. All of these factors contribute to simplifying deception on the Internet. In this section of the book we will therefore take a closer look at some key aspects of the manipulation of different types of digital content and senders on the Internet.

Recognise suspicious user accounts

It can be extremely difficult to establish who is behind a user account or website. Figures from the quarterly reports of Facebook and Twitter testify to the fact that a large number of user accounts on their platforms are not run by the person claiming to own the account. Both companies estimate, as stated, that around 5 per cent of all user accounts on their platforms are fake.

It is on the whole difficult to determine whether or not a user account on a social media platform is fake.[3] There are those who have attempted to create tools for this purpose, although none of these tools operates with a guarantee of a correct response, and the methods employed are controversial and subject to constant adaptation. Many of these tools are currently unavailable due to the frequent changes made to the APIs of social media platforms. Researchers at Indiana University have created a now defunct service called Botometer which anyone can use to assess the probability of a user account being a bot.[4] However, one of its administrators advises against using the tool to establish whether "individual accounts or groups of accounts are bots". It is best suited for assessing the relative impact of bots on given conversation topics.[5] Defined simply, the term "bot" here refers to a user account controlled by an algorithm that automatically produces content or interactions with other users. The same university's more advanced – and similarly defunct – software BotSlayer was designed for the needs of journalists and could disclose coordinated Twitter campaigns.[6] The results should nonetheless be taken with a grain of salt. The same holds true for news stories or other articles about large quantities of bots in which researchers or others have typically employed such tools.

Every journalist should nonetheless learn to recognise suspicious user accounts on major social media platforms, even without the help of technical tools. The organisation First Draft has compiled a list of red flags journalists should be aware of, on the basis of which I have created the following list.[7] If one or more of the criteria below is met, there is a chance that the user account is suspicious.

There may be cause for suspicion if the *user account*

- has been recently set up
- contains little or no personal information
- has a dubious, non-existent, stolen or computer-generated profile photo
- uses divisive rhetoric, hashtags, URLs or emojis in the bio
- has an obscure username – perhaps with many numbers or strange combinations of letters and numbers
- is copied, possibly from another social network
- follows many other accounts, has many followers and the number of both is approximately the same – or follows many accounts, but has no followers
- follows an odd mixture of user accounts (people on both ends of the US political spectrum is a recurring feature)
- is associated with other suspicious user accounts
- has disseminated dubious content previously
- has been previously flagged as suspicious by others.

There can be cause for suspicion if the *content*

- is published in different languages
- focuses on many international issues
- has features suggesting automation or that the user account is administrated by software (a recent example is the phrase “As an AI language model”)
- contains many provocative memes and animated content
- contains hashtags that are employed in a spam-like manner
- is sometimes off-brand
- has few links to credible sources

- has language that contains grammatical errors, seems somewhat odd and/or appears to have been generated by a translation app or a chatbot.

There can be cause for suspicion if the *activity*

- is high in terms of number of posts (typically more than 100 daily)
- is predominantly made up of shares (more than 80 per cent of the content)
- takes place both at night and during the day
- occurs only at specific times of day
- shows a dramatic increase or changes focus.

Motivations for manipulation

In recent years, the evolution of communication technology has generated new and far more effective methods for spreading false information to large groups of people in a short period of time.[8] One example of this would be social networks such as Facebook, where a large percentage of the world population has a user account. Research on the consequences of this development is nothing new, but the US presidential election of 2016 marked the start of a widespread public conversation about fictitious user accounts and manipulated internet content. Although these problems are as old as the Internet, these phenomena have experienced formidable growth in recent years. Between October 2017 and March 2023, Facebook took action on close to 30 billion fake user accounts – in many cases, allegedly before the accounts had the chance to become active.[9] In comparison, Facebook says that they have 2.9 billion active users each month, which attests to how widespread the attempts at manipulation are. Five per cent are, as we now know, fake user accounts, which on a global scale would constitute a minimum of 145 million fake Facebook accounts.

The activities of such user accounts are bought and sold openly online, and today it is wholly possible to purchase followers and interactions for every large-scale social media platform. The fake user accounts often stem from *click farms*, which use software, large quantities of cell phones and SIM cards to sell interactions from an army of cell phones and user accounts.[10] An investigation by *The New York Times* revealed that one sole company controlled around 3.5 million user accounts, which they sold to celebrities, brands and others who wanted to create the appearance of popularity through their online presence.[11] All told, the company had supplied more than 200 million Twitter followers to different user accounts.

The way social media functions makes it difficult to disclose the true identity of the sender of a message if this has been concealed. It is challenging to manually review all user accounts that have interacted with a webpage or social media post and subsequently make an assessment of the credibility of all of these. If it is a matter of hundreds of thousands of user accounts, this will require a great deal of time and resources. That is why most people don't question the figures reported by the social network itself.

The media regularly publicises social media content. To a large extent, in such cases the social platforms' own metrics, such as likes, followers and shares, are cited. This is data that is clearly visible on the user interface, is selected by the social medium in question, and is extremely difficult for outsiders to confirm. As such, using these figures as a basis for making a statement about reality, as journalists often do, is problematic. Urban studies scholar Jim Thatcher points out that researchers who use such data are accepting the commercialisation and quantification of knowledge.[12] Instead of fully reflecting the reality, our interactions with different platforms are actually the result of decisions taken by an extremely small group of programmers who work for private technology companies. Let's look at a typical example.

When a journalist covers a video that has had several million views, the fact that different social media and online platforms operate with extremely different definitions of what constitutes a view is seldom addressed. When we understand that manipulation occurs, that sometimes if the video was watched for a mere three seconds this is counted as a view, and that platforms such as Facebook have repeatedly reported inflated figures, it becomes clear that we cannot simply accept such claims at face value.[13]

There are many motives for creating and spreading false information and manipulated content on the Internet. In her book *Fake News*, Professor Bente Kalsnes specifies six such motives: technological, economic, political, military, social and psychological.[14] Based on experiences from the daily life of a journalist, the two predominant motivations outlined in this book are the economic and political:

Economic motivation: Swindling, fraud and other financial crimes are not new phenomena. A clear example of the immediate connection between such crimes and the media in recent times occurred during the US presidential election campaign in 2016. A large number of websites and Facebook pages appeared that published incorrect information. One of these was the website WTOE5News, which seemed to be an authentic US news site. It was only a few weeks old when it published one of the most discussed and erroneous news stories related to the election under the headline: "Pope Francis Shocks World, Endorses Donald Trump for President, Releases Statement".[15] The financial mechanisms behind such posts are not all that different from those we are familiar with from the press: create popular user accounts on social media, and drive traffic to a website using banner ads that generate advertising revenue. The more shocking the news, the greater the chances of high traffic volume and the corresponding profits. That was why in 2016 hundreds of websites about US politics, such as WTOE5News, were operated by teenagers based in the Macedonian city of Veles, who made a fortune on the sites.[16] It is not uncommon for well-known individuals or established media organisations to be exploited in online scam attempts. Fake news stories that appear to come from traditional media outlets, or programmes such as morning shows or talk shows, are examples of the ruses repeatedly employed in internet scam attempts. Links to these stories are typically spread through automated advertising platforms whereby they are posted on social media and even on the front pages of international and local online newspapers.

Political motivation: Neither are political propaganda and influence anything new. The Internet and social media today represent opportunities to spread political views inexpensively and effectively. Politicians, political stakeholders and even the military now use the Internet to exert influence. The threat assessment of the Norwegian Police Security Service from 2018 expressed an expectation that other nations would attempt to influence the public discourse and decision-making in Norway by way of "orchestrated information campaigns, through social media or deliberate leaks to Norwegian or international media channels".[17] This concern has been echoed in all the open threat assessments of Norwegian security and intelligence branches in the years since. Tools that can be employed for such purposes include click farms and troll factories that are active in many countries. Troll factories are enterprises or groups that spread content on the Internet in support of a given policy or political position – content that is also detrimental to the opposition. Any current news event can be exploited by these troll factories for the purpose of spreading false or manipulated information.

In 2020, Oxford Internet Institute found evidence of organised social media manipulation campaigns in 81 countries.[18] A somewhat modest analysis of the Norwegian municipal and county council elections of 2019 found no indication of foreign information manipulation in Norway, although other types of suspicious activity were disclosed.[19] The analysis does highlight how some stakeholders who are active in covert and extremist online forums moderate their activity on more public media and try to camouflage their attempts at active influence.[20] Actors who attempt to hide their connections to conceal a political agenda have been active on the Internet for many years.[21] In keeping with the technological development, the playing field has expanded from webpages and search engines to social media and other services.[22] Social media's inherent functions, such as the possibility for immediate response, are strategically exploited by users trying to hide a political agenda.[23]

Other attention-grabbing stunts are included in this broad category, even though their political motivation is not always immediately evident. Basically, any large-scale news event will attract the attention of digital troublemakers. The latter may be seeking to promote a cause or policy, provoke, poke fun and make mischief – a current event will often be exploited as a means of transmitting faulty or manipulated content. The more important the event, the more it will attract the attention of digital scam artists. Unfortunately, journalists will sometimes pick up false information and run with it, thereby furthering the dissemination of such content in the media.

Journalists as targets

The Internet is a journalistic goldmine, offering quick access to a wealth of sources – human interest stories and non-professional sources – in addition to sources of a professional and official nature. The diversity of content is vast, and traditionally journalists have been gatekeepers for their readers and viewers.

One of the challenges that arises due to so many of us being interconnected through social media is that we are all suddenly playing a key role in digital propaganda and disinformation attacks. Social media users are both the target of those wishing to exert influence and the tool employed to spread the message – simultaneously. All social media users should be aware of this. For journalists, one thing is certain: those who spread false information want journalists to create stories about their message. Media coverage opens the door to a far larger audience. Even fact-checking and the debunking of false claims are sought-after forms of coverage because they help spread the word.[24] As a journalist you should understand this and offer solid context whenever you make reference to false information. You should also be able to disclose and analyse networks of user accounts that spread incorrect claims or are engaged in covert, coordinated activity. This requires network analysis expertise, which we will cover later in this chapter of the book.

Journalists are exposed to both physical and digital security threats. This can be a matter of attempts to gain access to information journalists possess, but manipulation that affects journalists is also conducted on the Internet. Especially during ongoing news events, journalists became attractive targets. A US journalist who was reporting on a school shooting in Florida was made the target of manipulation and the spreading of altered tweets posted in such a way as to suggest that the journalist had inquired about a perpetrator's skin colour and requested photos of the murder victims, even though this was not the case.[25] Generally speaking, it is very simple to manipulate existing posts or create new posts on social media. Changing a website's source code will do, as will using one of countless websites that will allow you to generate posts, DMs, SMS or other forms of digital dialogue in a visually convincing manner. While it is becoming more difficult, until quite recently editing the headline or content and even doctoring the images used in articles and websites you have shared on social media has been a relatively simple task. It is indeed practical to be able to make small adjustments to text or to change an embedded image, as the social media platforms may have parsed the content of external websites incorrectly. However, it has become easier to change the headline of a news story entirely, and thereby present it in an entirely different light than originally intended.[26] Screenshots of news articles and other content can also be altered, though this is fortunately quite simple to disclose by tracking down the original article.[27] It is, however, more difficult to detect the manipulation of screen shots in cases where only minor elements from the article have been edited, such as copy from the body of the text.[28]

The value of manipulating a journalist

Based on the above, it is clear that journalists who do not critically evaluate digital sources constitute a potential goldmine for anyone aiming to acquire influence on the Internet. By failing to thoroughly check stories and causal inferences, you can end up drawing attention to and increasing the digital relevance of a story on the basis of faulty assumptions. Traditional media outlets today represent some of the most credible sites found online. Coverage by these established media outlets is coveted for marketing purposes and for garnering attention for a product, an idea or a website. This is absolutely nothing new historically speaking, but in the digital space it entails new and hidden consequences of which journalists should be aware. Search engines such as Google are constantly searching for links and connections on credible websites, to adjust and improve their recommendations and search results. A poor evaluation of sources on the part of an individual journalist for their own online newspaper can thus have consequences in wholly other realms of the Internet.

Google bombing

An attractive site on the Internet will have a high search engine result ranking. That is why Google can demand thousands of dollars per click on some advertisements linked to key search terms.[29] The algorithm PageRank was created by Google's founders (and named after one of them) and assigns a website a value based on the ranking of the websites linked to it. The greater the number of recognised websites that are linked to your page, the better the ranking of your page. There are also examples of manipulation of this algorithm. One such phenomenon is "Google bombing", in which a website is given an appearance of popularity through the creation of a large number of links to the site. By flooding the Internet with links to specific websites, the goal is to manipulate Google's algorithms and raise the ranking of these pages on the list of search results for specific key words or phrases.[30] Another phenomenon, known as "Google washing", involves the attempt to alter the search results displayed or push competitors down the list of search results for a given term.[31]

No follow*: maintaining critical distance in the digital domain*

When journalists reference a controversial phenomenon, false information or online scams, they automatically direct more traffic to this very content. Videos published on social media that would have otherwise gone virtually unnoticed can through media coverage attract an enormous number of viewers.[32] To offset this you can in certain cases anonymise a source to varying degrees. If you include links to a website as a journalist, you should be aware that this can influence the website's online reputation and improve its search engine and other types of rankings. Search engines will interpret links from media outlets as an endorsement. The linked site is thereby attributed a higher value, which can potentially lead to a much higher search result ranking.[33] You should therefore exercise caution when including links in your coverage.

If as a journalist you want to limit such a risk but nonetheless want to include a link, you can use the HTML tag rel="nofollow", which is a web standard indicating that your website does not endorse a link.[34] You can think of "nofollow" as a message to search engines that the link in your article is not to contribute to influencing their ranking of the page in question. This is, however, not a guarantee that the attention devoted to the page will be curbed. When *The New York Times* covered a fake campaign website for a presidential candidate, the journalist chose not to include the link, because the newspaper did not want to influence the page's ranking. The coverage alone nonetheless ensured that the site's ranking received a bump.[35]

The comment sections on pages with high credibility are a typical place where links are shared by visitors in hopes of achieving greater reach and a higher ranking for their site, but here "nofollow" is often automatically activated on all links. Google expanded the "nofollow" tag in 2019 to include a designated indicator for user-generated content (rel="ugc") and sponsored links (rel="sponsored").[36] Another alternative means of covering a website without linking to it is to take screenshots with clearly visible annotations and use these in news coverage. You can also consider whether the content itself is the most important part of the story, or if you should instead investigate it or those behind the website and cover the content in light of this information.

Wikipedia – for journalists

A source frequently used by the media is Wikipedia. The challenges related to this are best summarised by Wikipedia's own guidelines: "*You probably shouldn't be citing Wikipedia*".[37] Encyclopaedias are, after all, tertiary sources. As a journalist you should seek primary or first-hand sources and on a general basis critically assess all second- and third-hand sources. Wikipedia is moderated on a volunteer basis and anybody can contribute content, which means that not everything published there is necessarily accurate. Journalist Alex Pasternack nonetheless describes Wikipedia's volunteer moderators as the Internet's best weapon against false information, compared with other large web platforms that struggle to manage the large quantities of faulty information that comes their way.[38]

On Wikipedia, "co-authorship" is practised, which means that nobody owns the articles.[39] Because of this shared responsibility, all information must be critically evaluated by the reader. And most readers do: Norwegian research has shown that an overwhelming majority of schoolchildren know that the information found on Wikipedia can be incorrect.[40] In spite of this, Wikipedia is frequently used as a source in the Norwegian media. Because Wikipedia gathers information from other sources, citing the web encyclopaedia is in theory like citing information aggregators like Google or Statista. This is something you should avoid doing, because these platforms predominantly gather and present information from other sources.

As a journalist, you should primarily use Wikipedia articles as a source of general knowledge about the field of your investigation and to find other and better sources. If you nonetheless decide to cite Wikipedia articles, providing a link to them is a good practice. For accountability's sake, you should link to the version of the article as it appeared when you found the information. This is done by opening the heading *View history* and from there selecting the version with the most recent date on the list. In this way, both you and your readership gain access to an archive version of the article as it appeared when you cited it.

Wikipedia's list of revisions also gives you an indication of how many times the article has been edited and by whom. One of the most frequently revised articles in Wikipedia's history is the article about the war in Iraq. When collated in book form, the more than 12,000 changes fill 7,000 pages.[41] There are several articles containing thousands of revisions, which in its own right is a sign that you should approach the article with caution. Controversial facts or definitions are often rendered visible on an article's discussion page, while controversial or ambiguous questions are often apparent in the revision history.[42]

All revisions of a Wikipedia page are openly saved and connected to the user account or IP address responsible for implementing the revisions.[43] Journalists should be aware of this. This was how the Norwegian national daily newspaper *Dagens Næringsliv* could identify that Berit Kjøll, the then president of the Norwegian Confederation of Sports, had edited the Wikipedia article about herself and removed information about her previous involvement in a controversial matter.[44] If Kjøll had not registered in her own name, the IP address would have made it more difficult to trace the revision back to its source. Somebody else, of course, could have set up a user account in her name to make it appear as if Kjøll herself had made the change – and as a journalist you must be aware of all these contingencies and investigate before publishing any claims. It is not unusual to hear about individuals and enterprises who have edited information about themselves on Wikipedia. This is inadvisable, because it plants seeds of doubt about the neutrality of the content, a neutrality Wikipedia is rigorously endeavouring to uphold.

Twitter accounts such as @ParliamentEdits, @CongressEdits and various international versions send out a tweet every time an IP address registered at a parliamentary or governmental offices edits a Wikipedia page. They will nonetheless not capture all the changes made by the public authorities. If, say, a prime minister is connected to another network or has an anonymised username on Wikipedia, it will prove more difficult to detect any changes made by the head of state. As a journalist it is relevant to be aware that the update will be logged with your (or your employer's) IP address if you are not logged in when you make changes. Access to these changelogs is open on Wikipedia. The Twitter account @5thEstateWiki publishes a notification every time a computer used by a media organisation on their list publishes an update on Wikipedia without logging in.[45] For a registered user, only the username will be displayed.

Contributing to Wikipedia as a journalist

As a journalist, there is nothing to prevent you from contributing content to Wikipedia, as long as you follow the guidelines. After having worked on a story in depth, it is likely that you have accumulated credible information that would also be suitable content for Wikipedia articles on various topics. If you update an article by adding new information, the reference to your source must also be included. There are different ways of citing sources, but when citing basic information, footnotes work well. These can be included as metadata (data *about* data) throughout the text and can be automatically displayed in their entirety at the end of the article. It is relatively simple to create a reference to a website or an article. It is possible to include a number of types of information about the source, such as links to an archive version. Below you will find an example of a somewhat comprehensive reference on Wikipedia. It contains information about the type of source, the URL, the title of the work in question, author, publication date and place, a link to an archived version and information about whether you must be a subscriber to access the source:

```
<ref>{{cite news |last1=Tobiassen |first1=Markus|last2=Helle |first2=Birk Tjeldflaat |date=2019-05-06 |title=Fjernet egen rolle i Aker-konflikten fra Wikipedia |trans-title= Removed own role in the Aker conflict from Wikipedia |url=https://www.dn.no/pr/berit-kjoll/pr/norges-idrettsforbund/fjernet-egen-rolle-i-aker-konflikten-fra-wikipedia/2-1-615990 |url-access=subscription |language=Norwegian |work=Dagens Næringsliv |location=Oslo |access-date=2023-08-02 |archive-url= https://web.archive.org/web/20191101140702/https://www.dn.no/pr/berit-kjoll/pr/norges-idrettsforbund/fjernet-egen-rolle-i-aker-konflikten-fra-wikipedia/2-1-615990 |archive-date=2019-11-01|url-status=live |ref=none}}</ref>
```

If references are cited at the end of the article, this will ensure that all the footnotes appear there. If the citation is not embedded in the article, you can add a section containing references by writing the following at the bottom:

```
==References==
<references />
```

Wikidata

Key facts or figures can also be contributed to Wikidata, a database containing structured data used by Wikipedia and other websites. Information from Wikidata is typically displayed in Google's summaries of information linked to or at the top of search results. Let's take a look at an example. On Wikidata, under an entry about a company, you can add information about the number of employees, inform readers that the source category is an "official website", and add a hyperlink to the source and the year. Once the data item has been created, other pages on the Internet, such as Wikipedia's entries in different languages, will be able to reference this item through Wikipedia and other sites. When the item is updated on Wikidata, it will automatically be updated on all the other pages citing it as well.

Internet outrage and social media rows

Sometimes stories based on an internet event are given headlines such as "A sparks internet outrage" or "B triggers social media row". Stories of this nature make generalised claims based on inflammatory reactions to an event, citing a handful of such reactions as confirmation of the claims. The Swedish journalist Jack Werner uses the term "hate storm soup" to describe stories in which a few comments posted on the Internet are presented as evidence that someone is outraged.[46] Instead of finding an expert, a relevant source, a person to quote or speak with, the journalist uses online sources to represent the opinion of the people.[47]

An obvious challenge here is that finding corroboration for virtually any claim whatsoever on the Internet is easily accomplished. As an example, it does not take long to find a post on social media demonstrating that the UK prime minister is doing an excellent job. Or failing miserably. And this holds true for any topic whatsoever. Gathering a few, random opinions on a given issue and packaging them as an article by adding a few explanatory sentences requires very little effort. It is also lucrative, because it makes it possible to produce content rapidly. But these types of stories are problematic for a number of reasons.

On the surface, these types of stories appear to be digital "man on the street" interviews, but people on the Internet are *not* the same as people on the street. People on the street have a physical presence and are indisputably human beings. The Internet erases this kind of information about the sender, and far too often journalists will not go to the trouble of clarifying who has actually expressed the opinion or published the content on a platform and what they may be trying to achieve. It is very simple to set up an anonymous user account on social media, but the sender is attributed value and the relevance of the user account increased when journalists cite or embed content from a user account on social media directly on their media outlet's website. If the identity of the sender is not clearly specified, the reader will be obliged to abandon your story in order to access the user account you have cited to evaluate the sender's identity and integrity. Instead of investigating the digital sources to identify and clarify who has written the post, many media outlets frequently use descriptions such as "another [*insert social medium*] user" to designate the source when two or more social media posts are used to illustrate a view on a given issue.[48] If you don't evaluate a sender or user profile through use of digital source criticism, this can have serious consequences for your credibility, because you run the risk of being duped.

An example related to such "man on the street" interviews is a rhetorical device often employed by former US president Donald Trump. Instead of expressing an opinion, the former president says that "many people" say A, or believe B. "*Many people say that ...*" became one of Trump's signature phrases.[49] In this way, a controversial standpoint can be advocated even though, technically speaking, the president has not endorsed it.[50] The parallel to news stories exclusively based on social media posts is striking. With stories of this kind, journalists can spotlight fringe views on a flimsy basis. Using posts from social media in this manner as the core of a news story introduces problems at several levels:[51]

1. The news stories will be incorrect and/or shoddy.
2. Conscious or unconscious disinformation can easily seep into the media.
3. It contributes to legitimising a "*many people say*" discourse.

Although it is easy to find opinions on social media, as a journalist you should dig deeper into who says what and why. Research on how US journalists present tweets to their readers and viewers shows that this content is to a large extent allowed to speak for itself. The journalists reduce their role to that of a person who finds posts and disseminates them, but only to a limited extent verifies or otherwise applies journalistic methods to the content.[52]

It can be tempting to use a social media post as an example of something "many people say", but then it is important to remember how these platforms work. If 100 posts in support of a given viewpoint are written, this might create the impression that many users share this opinion. Still, 100 posts are not many when we know how frictionless and easily manipulated the digital (platform) landscape actually is. If 5 user accounts write posts on social media in support of a particular view, and a media outlet in Norway uses these posts as the backbone of a story, the public can easily gain the impression that this is the commonly accepted public opinion. But 5 users represent only 0.00009 per cent of the Norwegian population. Imagine that these user accounts were part of a propaganda network. It is obvious that the person or persons responsible will receive a great deal in return for their efforts if a media outlet helps spread the word to a large audience. Imagine, then, that there were 100,000 who actually wrote something. This would be experienced as an enormous storm on the Internet but still constitutes less than 2 per cent of the Norwegian population. Unfortunately, human beings in general are not proficient at evaluating the proportional significance of large numbers. Neither are journalists.

Undercover trolls: when the media takes the bait

The Russian Internet Research Agency (IRA) was long one of the most notorious troll factories in the world. Troll factories of this nature often employ user accounts on social networks to promote an agenda by assuming fictitious identities. Through so-called media hacking they also attempt to trick traditional media into disseminating false information.[53] This can occur through a flood of posts, comments, videos and pages on social networks and services such as Wikipedia. An example illustrating how successful such media hacking can be is a case from the presidential election of 2016, when a number of US media outlets, including *The Washington Post*, NPR and BuzzFeed, published tweets from user accounts stemming from the Russian Internet Research Agency (IRA).[54] The tweets were presented as the authentic US public opinion regarding the issue in question.

The phenomenon is international, and not really new. In 2007 journalism professor Rune Ottosen pointed out that the Norwegian media have no immune system in place to defend themselves against psychological warfare (so-called PSYOPS) of this kind.[55] Ottosen received the support of Norwegian newspaper editor Bjørgulv Braanen, who held that Norwegian media often failed to corroborate sources and used inadequate verification methods on information from international and especially US sources. The Norwegian national daily newspaper *Aftenposten*'s editor Harald Stanghelle stated that the Norwegian press were lacking in critical judgement, especially with regard to information from the large international news agencies, who can also be the victims of such psychological warfare.[56]

Almost a decade later, in the aftermath of the US presidential election of 2016, the US authorities revealed coordinated, manipulated activity on social media connected to the above-mentioned troll factory, Internet Research Agency. IRA had been active since the early 2010s, and its aim was to use the Internet to advance the political views of its clients. This manipulation was formerly limited to blogs and the comment sections of online newspapers, but with time migrated onto social media. After the 2016 presidential election, it was revealed that large and small media all over the world had cited and included content from these fictive user accounts in their articles.[57]

After having searched for several thousand usernames connected to this troll factory, which were publicised following the US authorities' investigation, I was able to establish that all major Norwegian media outlets had cited these fictive user accounts in their news coverage:[58] Twitter posts from fictive user accounts were cited by *VG*, *Dagbladet*, NRK, TV 2, *Aftenposten*, *Nettavisen* and *ABC Nyheter*. *Dagbladet* used a tweet from a fictive user account as an example of how the followers of French presidential candidate Marine Le Pen were the most active on Twitter during the 2017 presidential campaign. The tweet, which was included in *Dagbladet*'s article, claimed that a majority of the French police force had decided to vote for Le Pen ahead of the election.[59]

A solution in sight

There are a number of things journalists can do to avoid the problems that arise from handling content in this way. An obvious solution is to stop using random posts from social media as a source or the backbone of a news article. The best solution is to refrain from embedding social media posts directly into stories, and instead refer to, document and provide links to such posts after having verified their authenticity, along with the sender's. By taking screenshots of relevant content, you ensure that your story remains sound, even if the original post is deleted or revised after your story is published. It is tempting to embed some posts, because this can be a simple means of displaying media content such as images and video in a story. Still, this is not a good enough reason to jeopardise your own and your newsroom's credibility. Sometimes the identity of the source is relatively clear, but you should still investigate to determine whether the content, source and sender are in fact correct and credible or were originally published elsewhere online. Vague quantifiers, such as *many*, *some* and *hundreds*, should be given specificity to ensure the greatest amount of precision in the story.[60] This is particularly the case for digital content. Then the public can personally decide whether, say, 22 retweets actually constitutes "internet outrage".

If you come across interesting online content, you should track down the original source and contact the person who has written the post and get a quote instead. The drawback of this approach in a hectic workday is that it takes time. The upside is that if you make contact with a person whose name and other information correspond with the registered details for the user account, the likelihood of being deceived is substantially reduced. If an article or post is used nonetheless, you should make sure to provide sufficient context about the user and possibly why the post was written. If we evaluate digital sources to corroborate the identity of the person who has written a post, we avoid mistakes and the transmission of incorrect information.

Let us look briefly at three examples from the Norwegian Broadcasting Corporation (NRK) from 2019. In January, a Twitter post from a parody account set up in Progress Party politician Sylvi Listhaug's name was embedded and cited in an article as if it were authentic.[61] The same year, three anonymous Twitter accounts, Singapore Saint, Cousin Eddy and Barry #Boomer, were given a platform to voice their criticism of the prominent climate activist Greta Thunberg even though NRK did not know who was actually behind the user accounts.[62] The Twitter posts were later deleted from the story. Another example comes from NRK's coverage of the demonstrations in Hong Kong, at which time China's widespread digital influence campaign was disclosed.[63] A tweet containing a video purportedly showing violence from the demonstrations in Hong Kong from a user account with the username P0ZDLe70zxJtHVp was embedded in an article.[64] A quick check ascertained that the user account had been registered just a few days before, and had one follower and an edited profile photo of a Suzuki Swift car which was taken from a blog affiliated with a company that supplied a lowering kit for the car. As a journalist, you should instead locate the original source of the video you want to use. Based on the original source, you can find better, alternative means of transmitting the same video content to your audience.

Unearthing digital networks

One factor that makes it particularly challenging to effectively practise source criticism on the Internet is that the different social media platforms do not offer any simple means of investigating networks. Network analysis is a useful concept and tool because it allows us to pinpoint any connections between user accounts and clarify how content is disseminated online. Previously, automated user accounts attempting to promulgate different messages would pop up sporadically in response to large-scale news events. Today, this type of automated content is triggered by virtually every significant news story.[65]

As a journalist, you must consequently dig deep to disclose connections between a message and user accounts. Twitter was long been one of the most open social media platforms, which also made possible the extraction of data about the networks of user accounts. Facebook and Instagram, too, have shut down many of the opportunities to extract data about user accounts' networks, following a series of scandals related to data leaks and faulty enforcement of data protection. Blocking this type of access makes it more difficult for outsiders such as journalists to investigate user accounts and networks.

Although the procedure is a bit elaborate, it is not impossible to locate coordinated and covert activity on networks. It can be done manually, but this is extremely time-consuming. Another option is to extract data using a semi-automated process called webscraping. Some platforms have made it possible to extract data from APIs (the language computer programs use to communicate with each other). You can use computer programs to extract data from the platforms and process it using different tools.[66] Software such as NodeXL or the capture and analysis toolset 4CAT, developed by Digital Methods Initiative at the University of Amsterdam, enable you to do network analyses virtually without coding. By using one of these methods, you are better equipped to detect patterns and activity that is not visible in the ordinary use of platforms. This can be a matter of data about different words and themes, or user accounts and their behaviour: who they follow, who their followers follow, the message they are disseminating etc. It will also be possible to see how content such as a hashtag or link has migrated through the network. This is worth its weight in gold for a journalist who is going to explain why and how content has attracted attention on the Internet.

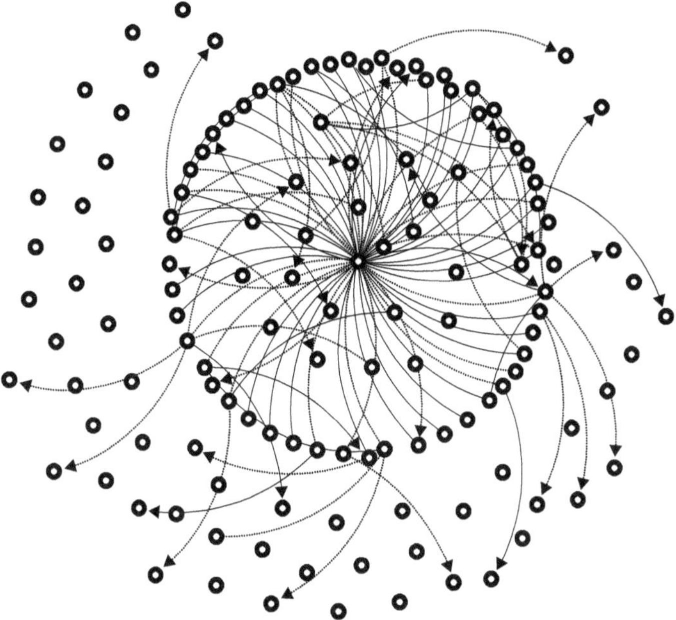

Figure 2.1 This is what a typical network analysis may look like.

With a little curiosity and basic skills from an online instructional video or a competent IT professional, it is possible to extract this kind of data – even though platforms are making it more difficult every day. The result is often a spreadsheet containing all the data, which can appear confusing. There are, fortunately, data visualisation tools available that can help with analysis and presentation. The program Gephi is popular for network visualisation because it functions on most platforms, has an open-source code and is free of charge.[67]

There are also simple techniques that you can use to investigate webpage networks in the same way as you would user accounts on social media. This can be done even if the webpage activity shows only a few traces of coordinated activity.

One method is to investigate the source code of a webpage to find identifiers. When you have opened the webpages' source code, you can search for "UA-". This is the start of the Google Analytics' tracking code which many websites have included because many websites use

Google Analytics. Archive versions of a webpage may also contain this code. When you have found the code, it is possible to do a reverse search using tools such as DNSlytics. This will disclose different websites that use this code and can provide critical hints about pages connected to the same Google Analytics account.[68]

Media manipulation

The amount of digital media content available on the Internet has increased dramatically over the past few decades. On the production end, a number of devices have been equipped with increasingly better cameras. Cell phones with camera technology for high-resolution photos and videos are now run of the mill. Cameras and sensors that allow for more advanced functions and perspectives are also common on more recent, state-of-the-art mobile phones. Increasingly smaller and better cameras and sensors are now included in satellites, cars, doorbells, surveillance equipment and sports gear. They are also included in other electronic devices that formerly have not had camera technology.

On the other end, the Internet is ready and able to receive the content produced by these cameras in large quantities. The content can be processed and edited in data cloud solutions, and immediately shared on social networks and a range of services. This means that anyone can produce high-quality documentation about anything, at any time. A consequence of this is that it becomes more important to be able to distinguish between credible and non-credible media content.

Journalism, along with the judicial system and the public authorities, has a need to ascertain the source and authenticity of digital media content.[69] One solution developed by scientists involves tools designed to investigate the manipulation of media content. At a technical level it is often a matter of identifying the different processes applied to a digital photo, both at the moment it was taken and after the fact. It is important to answer questions related to whether the content has been tampered with. Which image sensor captured the photo? In which camera is the sensor located? Databases such as Dresden Image Database contain photos taken in different scenarios, using different cameras, so researchers can identify small clues in the photos and disclose manipulation.[70] This is helpful for technicians who are going to perform advanced analyses, but far too time-consuming for a journalist in need of quick confirmation. There are, nonetheless, a number of investigations all journalists can carry out using simple methods.

Image and video manipulation

As we will explore in depth in Chapter 3, there are a number of precautions you must take before images and videos from the Internet can be used as credible documentation in journalism. We will first look at what journalists should know about the manipulation of visual media content. In their textbook about source criticism, Fossum and Meyer write that there is a widespread misconception that photography is a particularly credible source.[71] A photographer makes many decisions in the process of taking a photograph, each of which can have an impact on how the image turns out in the end. Using simple methods, a situation can be depicted in a specific way and for a specific purpose.[72] This means that photographs must also be subjected to evaluation and analysis, just like other sources. The many opportunities for the manipulation, alteration and creation of images through use of digital tools have spawned a certain general scepticism about photography as a source in our times, because seeds of doubt can be sown regarding veracity. Summing up photo manipulation is a long and convoluted process, and the phenomenon also has a long history, starting even before the digital image made it not only possible but simple for everyone to edit photos.

Image editing tools such as Photoshop have existed for over 30 years, and the general public has therefore acquired a certain awareness about how digital images, especially, can be manipulated. However, a similar awareness is not immediately apparent in the case of video. Because video content has become more common, it is virtually a law of nature that manipulated video content will also become more prevalent. It is therefore expedient to review the main techniques for image and video manipulation. Even though we are accustomed to thinking this way about photos, this is a reminder that all the video content we view may also have been manipulated in one way or another. The film industry has been doing so for decades, but the technology has become so effective and so cheap that anyone can produce convincing manipulations today.

Large news agencies such as Reuters have developed procedures and tools to disclose manipulated content. After a scandal in 2007, when the agency disseminated manipulated images from a freelance journalist, Reuters was obliged to update its routines.[73] This work was escalated in 2019 to meet new challenges. The agency established guidelines, training programmes and procedures for detecting the advanced manipulation of video content, known as *deepfakes*.[74] Deepfakes can be defined as media content that has been corrupted or created using machine learning technology. Examples usually include manipulation of existing videos; the technology is used to make it appear as if someone has said or done something they have never said or done. The challenge for all media and journalists is to update their guidelines and knowledge continuously and in step with technological advancements. It is likely, however, that a perpetual game of cat and mouse will continue in the future between those who manipulate media content and those who endeavour to disclose it.

In a wholly fundamental sense, the most important means of preventing the dissemination of manipulated photos and images in the media is to increase the newsroom's overall awareness about the different existing types of manipulation. We will address the primary methods used to manipulate media content to illustrate the broad range of techniques that can be used. At one end of this spectrum, we find media content that has not been manipulated but nonetheless can be misleading or erroneous because angles and contextual information have been omitted or altered. At the other end, we find digitally manipulated content, such as videos that have been tampered with or created through use of special software and machine learning.

It is not difficult to understand how easy it is to present an unedited image or video online as something other than what it actually is, solely through reliance on an incorrect or missing context. Sophisticated manipulation of content is actually not necessary, because it is very simple to spread something that is wholly authentic in a manner that is misleading. The origin of an image or a video, allegedly depicting a natural disaster that has just occurred, can in fact be from an event that took place many years ago. A statement issued by a politician may have been made in a wholly different context than the situation presented. Shocking documentation of something which has just taken place will easily attract a lot of attention and is in demand by media all over the world. If the media publishes inaccurate content, this means that inaccurate information is conveyed to a large number of people. Then it makes little difference that one was first to break the story. Although manipulation can be wholly banal, such as an altered

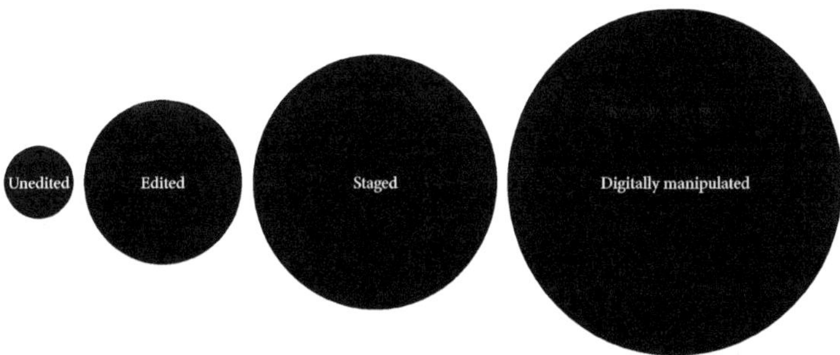

Figure 2.2 Manipulated photo and video content can be broken down into four main categories: unedited, edited, staged and digitally manipulated. The latter requires the greatest amount of resources.

subtitle or graphic overlay on a video, the content can nonetheless spread like wildfire on the Internet.[75] Modern social media, often called digital platforms, must shoulder some of the blame for this. The large platforms have few technical or structural incentives for practising source criticism or even including information about sources when sharing content. The evaluation of sources takes time, which jars with the large social networks' visions of quick and frictionless consumption of content.

Since a large variety of methods for image and video manipulation exist, it is unrealistic to expect every journalist to be an expert on all of them. Newsrooms should therefore develop healthy instincts in the critical evaluation of all media content and understand the opportunities that lie in the different techniques and methods for manipulation of such content. Armed with knowledge about digital source criticism, and perhaps some assistance from technical tools, you will be well equipped to detect manipulated media content. The following basic categories encompass the majority of the digital image and video manipulation techniques found today.

Unedited media

Even if media content has not been edited, this does not mean that it can be trusted. Content which, technically speaking, has not been tampered with can communicate incorrect information because it presents an incident from solely one camera angle or documents a single, isolated event from a larger, extended sequence. Images can also be presented as if they occurred in another situation altogether. The manipulation lies in taking the content, or parts of it, out of the original context. If content is disseminated online with a misleading description or without relevant contextual information, it can end up misrepresenting the actual events. A recurring example is how videos from military drills, demonstrations of different types of weapons, or old conflict footage are presented as actual footage of ongoing conflicts.

A well-known example of misleading through misrepresentation occurred when the president of France shared a Twitter post in August of 2019, a period during which there were widespread forest fires in the Amazon rainforest. The post included a photo which purportedly depicted the Amazon on fire. Although it was not explicitly stated that the image was current, a buzz was created when it turned out that the photo had not been taken recently. The news agency AFP was unable to establish exactly when the photo was taken, but because the photographer died in 2003, we can conclude that the photo must have been taken at least 16 years before the president shared it.[76]

In January 2019, a confrontation in front of the Lincoln Monument between a 16-year-old student wearing a MAGA cap and an elderly indigenous people's activist was filmed in the US. An unedited video clip of the altercation was spread on social media and quickly attracted the attention of large media outlets internationally. Although the clip was not edited, it still gave a false impression of the actual events. A common feature of such unedited clips is that they often lack documentation of what happened before a situation, or the camera angle obscures one or more critical detail of importance. After having used a single video as a source, US media outlets such as *The Washington Post*, along with *VG*, TV 2 and NRK in Norway, were obliged to correct their own coverage when several more videos of the same incident surfaced online.[77] *The Washington Post* writes that the additional video documentation made it possible for them to carry out a more comprehensive assessment of what had actually taken place.[78] A good rule of thumb is therefore to try and find further documentation, more photos and videos *before* proceeding with coverage of sensational content. In short, even if media content has not been tampered with, it can still convey an incorrect impression of a situation. Coupled with the desire for rapid response in news coverage, there is a high risk of error associated with the use of isolated video clips.

Edited media

Even a simple edit can dramatically alter the content of photos and videos. For videos, simple edits are often made, such as removing the beginning or ending of an event. A clip can also be combined with other video clips or excerpts from the same clip and thereby alter the perception of the events. Videos of this nature are often referred to as *cheapfakes* because they are cheap and easy to make, or *shallowfakes* because the methods used to create them are basic and rudimentary. The playback speed of a video can be accelerated or slowed down, either for short sequences or throughout the entire clip, to make it appear as if something else altogether has happened. This type of manipulation can be easily detected by getting hold of the unedited, original version of the video. Headlines were made all over the world when a doctored video of the US politician Nancy Pelosi appeared on Facebook.[79] Because the footage had been slowed down, Pelosi appeared to be intoxicated or ill, but if the video is viewed beside the original, it is easy to establish that this was not the case.

Image manipulation is, as stated, very simple and inexpensive to do today. Using tools such as Photoshop, anything can be done to a photograph, but a commonality of edited images related to news events is often that elements have either been removed or added to the photo. There are plenty of examples of press photos and photos from conflict zones that have been edited and subsequently reproduced by traditional media. In the case of the Reuters scandal mentioned above, the photographer had edited the image to make it appear more sensational by adding additional and more dramatic smoke.[80] The more images or videos you have access to from the same place and from separate sources, the better your chances of discovering whether media content has been edited.

Staged media

Fabricated content, both with and without context, appears on the Internet on a regular basis. Removing or concealing context to obscure the fact that an event was orchestrated or purely fictional, and presenting the documentation as real, can lead to rapid dissemination of content of this nature. The likelihood of this occurring is compounded if the staged content is presented as if it were related to a current event or occurred at the same moment as another dramatic incident. In this way, a military drill captured on film, a humorous video, or video footage of an emergency service demonstration can be presented as an actual rescue mission. In such cases, high-quality footage can be an indication of solid preparation and should prompt caution on the part of journalists reporting on such content. A staged video of Croatian firefighters who appear to be responding to an emergency call just seconds before a decisive penalty kick at the football World Cup went viral and was transmitted by ABC News, among other news outlets, as actual footage.[81]

One of the most well-known examples of such a staged video in recent years is "Syrian Hero Boy", which was published on YouTube and attracted millions of views along with a great deal of attention elsewhere on the Internet and on social media.[82] In the video, a child runs to the rescue of another child and becomes the target of sniper fire. The rescuing child (*hero boy*) appears to be shot. Then the surprise comes. The child gets to his feet and escapes, running away with the other child while spectators cheer them on. The situation appears to be an authentic event from the civil war in Syria, but, in reality, was a video filmed in Malta by the Norwegian director Lars Klevberg, in conjunction with a project made possible through funding from the Norwegian Film Institute and Arts and Culture Norway. When it was disclosed that the video was staged, there was an onslaught of criticism and an apology was subsequently issued.[83]

Digitally manipulated media

The umbrella term "digitally manipulated content" can be broken down into a number of subcategories. For videos, the common feature is animation, typically done using computer technology. Terms such as computer-generated imagery (CGI), visual effects (VFX) or "deepfakes" are recurring. Professional film and television communities have long created credible digital manipulation, but because the technology used to produce such videos has become more accessible and cheaper, this type of manipulation is also finding its way into ordinary computers, mobile phones and apps. Relatively widespread video editing tools such as Adobe's Premiere have also acquired the functionality we are familiar with from photo editing programs such as Photoshop. With the help of a few commands, it is now possible to use such tools to remove or add elements to a video. Other tools promise to generate entire video scenes based on text input alone.

Although simple manipulation methods can be extremely effective, deepfakes have received a lot of media and scholarly attention. As stated, deepfakes are manipulated media content that is generated using machine learning and can be produced on ordinary computers. With sufficient training data, such as thousands of photos of a person, new elements, such as faces, people or objects, can be manipulated into existing videos in a credible fashion. The fear is that the technology will be used to promote falsified messages from politicians or become so widespread that it will be virtually impossible to determine what has actually been said. The results from the use of this technology are for the time being not particularly credible, but as is the case for a lot of other technology, deepfakes are undergoing rapid development and improvement.

There are many examples of digitally manipulated videos that have gone viral. An example of digital manipulation of an authentic video is a snowboarder who films herself on the way down a mountainside while wearing headphones that are blasting music. In the viral video we can see that, unbeknownst to the snowboarder, she is being chased by a bear. The bear was added after the fact.[84] Several deepfake videos have been created based on videos of presidents such as Putin and Obama, and the fear is that such videos could trigger real-world conflicts. Professor Hany Farid outlines a scenario in which a video of the US president announcing a nuclear attack on North Korea is released on social media. The video goes viral and provokes an immediate counterattack on the part of North Korea.[85] For the time being, however, deepfakes are commonly used to create pornographic content by overlaying images of both famous and unknown people, usually women, on existing video footage.[86] A number of video-sharing websites and social media platforms have therefore prohibited or implemented restrictions on this type of digitally manipulated content.

There are not many examples of wholly computer-generated images that have fooled the press, but we are on the brink of a new era. Advanced photo manipulation can now be done on mobile phones, whereby elements in a photo can be altered or replaced.[87] Apps that can change the sky in photos can immediately present a rainy day as full of sunshine instead. One face can be easily replaced by another.

A hint of the future development is the use of machine learning to generate fictive profile photos. The machine learning technology is the same as that which led to the phenomenon of deepfakes, but it can also be used to generate photos. There are websites and services that can generate an infinite number of unique photos that look like a typical profile photo of a human being.[88] The technology behind this has "learned" what a profile photo looks like by studying patterns and recurring features in thousands of actual profile photos. It is subsequently able to reproduce these patterns in new ways and thereby generate a new human face. The pictures are extremely credible, especially if they are shown in a small profile photo format on a mobile phone display, but for the time being, we can with relative facility detect irregularities and inconsistent details in the hair, mouth or eyes in a high-resolution version of such images. Eyeglasses further increase the complexity, and photos with eyeglasses are therefore seldom used. Incredible advancements have been made in just a few years on the creation of such fabricated images, and it is now challenging to distinguish them from real photographs – especially if displayed on small screens. There are cases of such computer-generated profile photos being used to fool journalists, among others. In one example, someone used a fictive name and computer-generated profile photo to impersonate a credible Norwegian social commentator and assumed this identity in public and private communication with many prominent media figures.[89]

Audio manipulation

Unfortunately, there are not many bright spots when it comes to detecting audio manipulation. Audio experts claim that it is extremely difficult, even for someone with special expertise in the field, to disclose manipulation.[90] Although this area of expertise is generally beyond the scope of what can be expected from a journalist, it is nonetheless useful to be aware of both the possibilities and limitations in order to effectively evaluate the sources of audio content. We will therefore dive briefly into audio manipulation and the detection techniques available to the average journalist.

Not surprisingly, when it comes to audio, the machine learning technology covered in the section "Image and video manipulation" also pertains here. Adobe, responsible for programs such as Photoshop, years ago demonstrated a prototype called Voco that could manipulate an audio recording of human speech merely by editing text.[91] With access to a 20-minute recording of a human voice, the program could make that voice say anything at all in an extremely credible fashion. The potential for abuse is clearly substantial and may have been why Adobe never launched the program. But Adobe is not the only stakeholder working on audio manipulation in this way. A service for podcast editing called Descript offers to create a model of your own voice and lets you manipulate the audio by editing text in a manuscript.[92] In 2023 Apple released a feature called Personal Voice in their mobile operating system that allows anyone to create a digital clone of their voice that can be controlled via text input. The message behind these examples is that the manipulation of audio will not become less widespread or easier to detect in the future. In May 2019, computer-generated audio clips of podcast host Joe Rogan appeared on the Internet that were extremely convincing. They were created by a start-up company within the field of machine learning.[93] Attempted scams have already been reported, including one in which a synthetic voice clip imitating the speech of a company director was used to deceive employees over the telephone.[94]

Manipulated, synthetic or incorrect audio content created to fool the media and others is for the time being not highly prevalent on the Internet, but cases are increasing. In connection with the COVID-19 virus, an audio clip was disseminated using the messaging service WhatsApp. In the clip you can hear a person claiming to be an ambulance worker in the UK. The person divulges shocking details that had purportedly been shared at a recent work meeting and claims that before long a large number of children will become sick and the healthcare system will collapse. The UK healthcare authorities issued assurances that the alarming information on the recording was incorrect and advised the public to ignore it.[95]

For journalists today, analysis of audio is closely tied up with the work of analysing manipulated videos.[96] Journalists should be aware of the different issues related to audio recordings, even though advanced manipulation of such material can really only be properly analysed by audio technology experts. Without a specially designed audio recorder that generates a unique and verifiable code (a kind of digital fingerprint called a *hash*), the moment the audio recording is concluded it is not possible to prove its authenticity.[97] It is therefore important to get as close to the digital source as possible, following the procedure outlined in Chapter 3. The closer you are to a file's digital origin, the better equipped you will be to analyse the file's credibility. As soon as the file is processed by a program or a web service, significant details can be erased.

In the manipulation of a voice recording, the possibilities for cutting and splicing are limited. Cuts must be made between words, for example, to avoid disclosing manipulation. If breathing is cut, this can easily be heard. A technique journalists can use is to analyse background noises. Do sudden changes occur in the background sounds that cannot be explained by a natural event? Is there a radio or fan on in the background and, if so, does the sound produced change suddenly?

An exciting example of how it is possible to extract information that can be hidden in background noise is described by researcher Catalin Grigoras. The method in question utilises low-frequency background sounds that are generated by the power grid and often appear on audio recordings.[98] The powerline frequency in Norway is 50 Hz but fluctuates slightly. Our power grids "live" because many large and small machines are started up and shut down, but not simultaneously. In the course of a particular time frame it is therefore possible to establish a type of audio fingerprint for the 50 Hz frequency that is unique for a given place at a specific time. With information from the company that operates the power grid, this can be subsequently confirmed. The result is that experts can in some cases establish the time and place of an audio recording's origin on the basis of information from the power grid.[99]

Digital tools for the analysis of audio are both easily available and often free of charge, but the challenge is that you must know how to use the software and what to look for. Basically, what audio technicians do to analyse audio clips is to search for traces of changes. Although the police do not wish to share their work methods in detail, some tips and advice are available that can be helpful for journalists when it comes to disclosing the potential manipulation of audio clips:

- What are people saying on the recording? Is there a natural connection between what they are saying and the other descriptions of the content?
- Is the language being spoken consistent?
- Are accents and dialects consistent with the region from which the content supposedly originates?
- Are there strange cuts in words and natural breathing sounds?
- If you hear something suspicious, visualise the sound as a spectrogram and look for irregularities in the background noises.
- Listen for things such as fans, traffic or a radio in the background. Do sudden and inexplicable changes in the background sound occur?

- Does the audio correspond with the image you have of the situation? Is something happening in the background? If something is taking place, it would be logical to expect to hear this too.
- If you have the original file, what does the Exif data say? If you find codes such as “Soundforge 5.0” or “Logic”, the file has been processed by audio editing software.

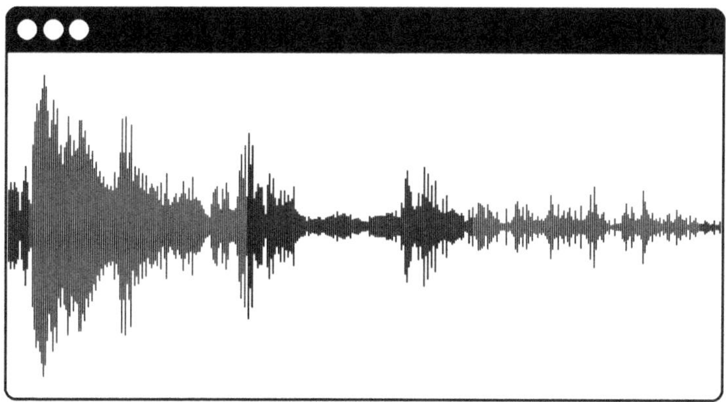

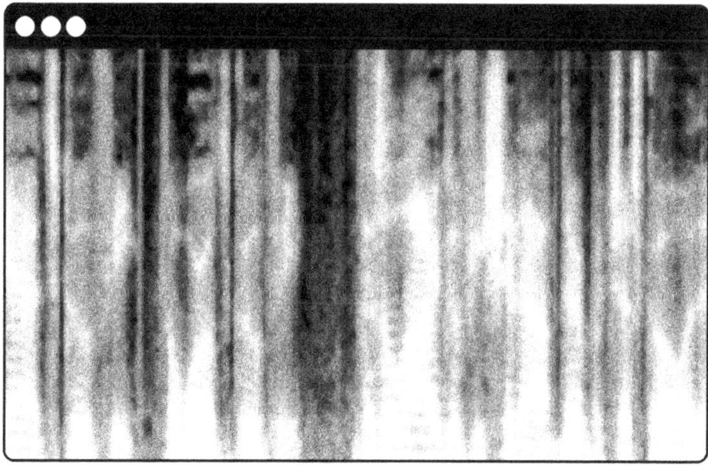

Figure 2.3 An audio clip visualised in wave form (above) and a spectrogram (below) in the software Adobe Audition.

Questions for reflection and exercises

- Check the sources of some foreign coverage in large local media outlets. Are there any social media posts found among these? Analyse the post's sender. Is it probable that the journalist has carried out a proper evaluation of the user account before publication?
- Set up a news category search for the names of some social networks such as Instagram, Facebook and Twitter through Google Alerts. What recurring media and user accounts appear?
- Find Wikipedia articles about individuals or enterprises, perhaps within the media, the business world or technology. Access the revisions log and look for signs indicating that they have written or revised the article themselves. What do you find?
- Use a network analysis tool like Hoaxy to analyse a popular web article from the past week. What can you find out about the network and how the article has been disseminated?
- Have you seen or discovered any examples of manipulated media content in the past week? What are the stories about? How is the content discussed by different media outlets?

Notes

1 Ipsos, *Ipsos SoMe-tracker Q2'23* (8 August 2023). Retrieved 23 October 2023 from Ipsos ipsos.com/sites/default/files/ct/publication/documents/2023-08/Ipsos%20SoMe-tracker%20Q2%202023.pdf

2 Meta, *Meta Earnings Presentation Q2 2023* (26 July 2023). Retrieved 23 October 2023 from Meta Investor Relations s21.q4cdn.com/399680738/files/doc_financials/2023/q2/Earnings-Presentation-Q2-2023.pdf

3 Siobhan Roberts, *Who's a Bot? Who's Not?* (16 June 2020). Retrieved 17 October 2020 from New York Times nytimes.com/2020/06/16/science/social-media-bots-kazemi.html

4 Available at botometer.iuni.iu.edu

5 Morgan Meaker, *This Student's Side Project Will Help Decide Musk vs. Twitter* (27 November 2022). Retrieved 2 august 2023 from Wired www.wired.co.uk/article/musk-twitter-botometer

6 Observatory on Social Media, *Botslayer* (2019). Retrieved 6 December 2019 from Indiana University osome.iuni.iu.edu/tools/botslayer

7 Carlotta Dotto & Sebastien Cubbon, *How to spot a bot (or not): The main indicators of online automation, co-ordination and inauthentic activity* (28 November 2019). Retrieved 6 December 2019 from First Draft firstdraftnews.org/latest/how-to-spot-a-bot-or-not-the-main-indicators-of-online-automation-co-ordination-and-inauthentic-activity

8 Srijan Kumar & Neil Shah, *False Information on Web and Social Media: A Survey* (23 April 2018). Retrieved 17 April 2020 from arXiv:1804.08559 (cs) arxiv.org/abs/1804.08559

9 Facebook, *Community Standards Enforcement Report* (May 2023). Retrieved 2 August 2023 from Facebook Transparency Centre transparency.fb.com/data/community-standards-enforcement/fake-accounts/facebook

10 Sean Mantesso, *'A room full of 20-year-old men smoking': What is a click farm, and how do they make money?'* (30 March 2019). Retrieved 16 April 2020 from ABC News abc.net.au/news/2019-03-30/farming-for-likes-fake-social-media-engagement/10944078

11 Nicholas Confessore et al., *The Follower Factory* (27 January 2018). Retrieved 17 April 2020 from The New York Times nytimes.com/interactive/2018/01/27/technology/social-media-bots.html

12 Jim Thatcher, *Living on Fumes: Digital Footprints, Data Fumes, and the Limitations of Spatial Big Data* (2014). International Journal of Communication, 8, 19. Retrieved 4 September 2020 from ijoc.org/index.php/ijoc/article/view/2174

13 John Herrman & Sapna Maheshwari, *Facebook Apologizes for Overstating Video Metrics* (23 September 2016). Retrieved 15 April 2020 from The New York Times nytimes.com/2016/09/24/business/media/facebook-apologizes-for-overstating-video-metrics.html

14 Bente Kalsnes, *Fake news [Falske nyheter]* (2019). Cappelen Damm Akademisk.

15 Craig Silverman & Jeremy Singer-Vine, *The True Story Behind The Biggest Fake News Hit Of The Election* (16 December 2016). Retrieved 14 April 2020 from BuzzFeed News buzzfeednews.com/article/craigsilverman/the-strangest-fake-news-empire

16 Craig Silverman & Lawrence Alexander, *How Teens In The Balkans Are Duping Trump Supporters With Fake News* (3 November 2016). Retrieved 14 April 2020 from BuzzFeed News buzzfeednews.com/article/craigsilverman/how macedonia-became-a-global-hub-for-pro-trump-misinfo

17 Norwegian Police Security Service (Politiets sikkerhetstjeneste), *Threat assessment 2018 [Trusselvurdering 2018]* (30 January 2018). Retrieved 15 April 2020 from PST pst.no/trusselvurdering-2018

18 Samantha Bradshaw & Philip N. Howard, *Industrialized Disinformation: 2020 Global Inventory of Organized Social Media Manipulation* (February 2020). Retrieved from Oxford Internet Institute demtech.oii.ox.ac.uk/wp-content/uploads/sites/12/2021/02/CyberTroop-Report20-Draft9.pdf

19 Tor Olav Grøtan et al., *In search of foreign information influence [På leting etter utenlandsk informasjonspåvirkning]* (28 November 2019). Retrieved 15 April 2020 from Regjeringen regjeringen.no/no/dokumenter/pa-leting-etter-utenlandsk-informasjonspavirkning/id2686450

20 Tor Olav Grøtan et al., *New report: Did foreign actors influence the Norwegian election in 2019? [Ny rapport: Påvirket utenlandske aktører det norske valget i 2019?]* (27 February 2020). Retrieved 15 April 2020 from Agenda Magasin agendamagasin.no/debatt/rapport-pavirket-utenlandske-aktorer-norske-valget

21 Jessie Daniels, *Cloaked websites: Propaganda, cyber-racism and epistemology in the digital era* (2009). New Media & Society doi.org/10.1177/1461444809105345

22 Johan Farkas, Jannick Schou & Christina Neumayer, *Cloaked Facebook pages: Exploring fake Islamist propaganda in social media* (2018). New Media & Society, 20(5), 1850–1867 doi.org/10.1177/1461444817707759

23 Ibid.

24 Claire Wardle, *5 Lessons for Reporting in an Age of Disinformation* (27 December2018).Retrieved21November2019fromFirstDraftfirstdraftnews.org/latest/5-lessons-for-reporting-in-an-age-of-disinformation

25 Daniel Funke, *Imposter tweets made it even harder for a reporter to cover Florida school shooting* (15 February 2018). Retrieved 26 October 2019 from Poynter poynter.org/fact-checking/2018/imposter-tweets-made-it-even-harder-for-a-reporter-to-cover-florida-school-shooting

26 Gard L. Michalsen, *Centre Party created their own alternative angle when they shared a news article from Dagbladet on Facebook [Senterpartiet laget sin egen alternative vinkling da de delte en nyhetssak from Dagbladet på Facebook* (2 March 2017). Retrieved 21 November 2019 from Medier24 medier24.no/artikler/senterpartiet-lagde-sin-egen-alternative-vinkling-da-de-delte-en-nyhetssak-fra-dagbladet-pa-facebook/377413

27 Ståle Grut, *Fake headlines from Norwegian media outlets are shared on Facebook [Falske overskrifter from norske medier deles på Facebook]* (9 December 2016). Retrieved 26 October 2019 from NRKbeta nrkbeta.no/2016/12/09/falske-overskrifter-fra-norske-medier-deles-pa-facebook

28 Daniel Funke, *Fake Miami Herald screenshots are stoking fears of more school threats* (22 February 2018). Retrieved 26 October 2019 from Poynter poynter.org/fact-checking/2018/fake-miami-herald-screenshots-are-stoking-fears-of-more-school-threats

29 Jim Leichenko, *The Most Expensive Keywords on Google – Anniversary Edition* (4 September 2018). Retrieved 9 September 2019 from Kantar Media kantarmedia.com/us/thinking-and-resources/blog/adg-the-most-expensive-keywords-on-google-anniversary-edition

30 Tom Zeller Jr., *A New Campaign Tactic: Manipulating Google Data* (26 October 2006). Retrieved 21 November 2019 from The New York Times nytimes.com/2006/10/26/us/politics/26googlebomb.html

31 Andrew A. Adams & Rachel J. McCrindle, *Pandora's Box: Social and Professional Issues of the Information Age* (2008), John Wiley & Sons, pp. 122–123.

32 Facebook's former head of security and current director of Stanford Internet Observatory: Alex Stamos on Twitter: "This is a pattern we saw with both the Christchurch and Pelosi-cheapfake videos. The mass media coverage of terrorist content or disinformation has the effect of driving 10x the traffic that might occur organically. " (29 June 2019). Retrieved 11 September 2019 from Twitter twitter.com/alexstamos/status/1145075357369786368

33 Matthew Rosenberg, *Trump Consultant Is Trolling Democrats With Biden Site That Isn't Biden's* (29 June 2019). Retrieved 11 September 2019 from The New York Times nytimes.com/2019/06/29/us/politics/fake-joe-biden-website.html

34 WHATWG, *HTML Standard–4.6.6.11 Link type "nofollow"* (9 September 2019). Retrieved 11 September 2019 from HTML Living Standard–Last Updated 9 September 2019 html.spec.whatwg.org/multipage/links.html#link-type-nofollow

35 Victoria Kwan, *When does reporting become a megaphone for disinformation?* (14 August 2019). Retrieved 11 September 2019 from First Draft firstdraftnews.org/when-does-reporting-become-a-megaphone-for-disinformation

36 Danny Sullivan & Gary Illyes, *Evolving "nofollow" – new ways to identify the nature of links* (10 September 2019). Retrieved 24 September 2019 from Official Google Webmaster Central Blog webmasters.googleblog.com/2019/09/evolving-nofollow-new-ways-to-identify.html

37 Specifically, it was the user Moxy who made this statement in this revision of Wikipedia's guidelines for how to cite Wikipedia: *Citing Wikipedia* (23 December 2016). Retrieved 12 September 2019 from Wikipedia en.wikipedia.org/w/index.php?title=Wikipedia:Citing_Wikipedia&oldid=756384087

38 Alex Pasternack, *How Wikipedia's volunteers became the web's best weapon against misinformation* (7 March 2020). Retrieved 12 April 2020 from Fast Company fastcompany.com/90471667/how-wikipedia-volunteers-became-the-webs-best-weapon-against-misinformation

39 Harald Groven, *"Digital literacy" 26 May in Stavanger ["Digital kompetanse" 26. mai i Stavanger]* (27 May 2016). Retrieved 10 September 2019 from Prezi prezi.com/ufhizi8mfdyk/digital-kompetanse-26-mai-i-stavanger

40 Marte Blikstad-Balas, *"You get what you need": A study of students' attitudes towards using Wikipedia when doing school assignments* (2016). Scandinavian Journal of Educational Research, 60(6), 594–608 doi.org/10.1080/00313831.2015.1066428

41 James Bridle, *On Wikipedia, Cultural Patrimony, and Historiography* (6 September 2010). Retrieved 10 September 2019 from Booktwo booktwo.org/notebook/wikipedia-historiography

42 Harald Groven (former board member of Wikipedia Norway), personal communication, 10 September 2019.
43 Harald Groven, *"Digital literacy" 26 May in Stavanger ["Digital kompetanse" 26. mai i Stavanger]* (27 May 2016). Retrieved 10 September 2019 from Prezi prezi.com/ufhizi8mfdyk/digital-kompetanse-26-mai-i-stavanger
44 Markus Tobiassen & Birk Tjeldflaat Helle, *Removed own role in the Aker conflict from Wikipedia [Fjernet egen rolle i Aker-konflikten from Wikipedia]* (05 June 2019). Retrieved 10 September 2019 from Dagens Næringsliv dn.no/pr/berit-kjoll/pr/norges-idrettsforbund/fjernet-egen-rolle-i-aker-konflikten-fra-wikipedia/2-1-615990
45 Christopher Isene, *MediaCreeper–About* (undated). Retrieved 23 September 2019 from MediaCreeper mediacreeper.com/index
46 Jack Werner, *How many comments creates a storm of hatred? [Hur många kommentarer utgör en hatstorm?]* (2 December 2019). Retrieved 16 April 2020 from Dagens Nyheter dn.se/kultur-noje/jack-werner-hur-manga-kommentarer-utgor-en-hatstorm
47 A search for news using the word "Twitter" will quickly provide examples. The phenomenon is precisely described by Ranjan Roy in *The Rule of 140* (20 July 2019). Retrieved 4 September 2019 from the newsletter The Margins themargins.substack.com/p/the-rule-of-140
48 Do a search on Google News using "[insert social media]-user*" to retrieve the most recent cases. A search of the same site using "twitter" demonstrates how often the platform is cited or used as a source in Norwegian media: numerous times in the course of a given 24-hour period.
49 Nancy L. Rosenblum & Russell Muirhead, *A Lot of People Are Saying: The New Conspiracism and the Assault on Democracy* (2019), Princeton University Press, p. 3.
50 Jenna Johnson, *'A lot of people are saying ... ': How Trump spreads conspiracies and innuendoes* (13 June 2016). Retrieved 4 September 2019 from *Washington Post* washingtonpost.com/politics/a-lot-of-people-are-saying-how-trump-spreads-conspiracies-and-innuendo/2016/06/13/b21e59de-317e-11e6-8ff7-7b6c1998b7a0_story.html
51 Ranjan Roy, *The Rule of 140* (20 July 2019). Retrieved 4 September 2019 from the newsletter The Margins themargins.substack.com/p/the-rule-of-140
52 Logan Molyneux & Shannon McGregor, *Think twice before turning to Twitter* (31 December 2019). Retrieved 12 January 2020 from Nieman Lab niemanlab.org/2019/12/think-twice-before-turning-to-twitter
53 Øystein Bogen, *Putin and I [Putin og jeg]* (2017). Kagge Forlag, Oslo, p. 400.
54 Tony Romm & Rani Molla, *The Washington Post, Miami Herald, InfoWars and other U.S. sites spread Russian propaganda from Twitter* (3 November 2017). Retrieved 5 November 2019 from Recode vox.com/2017/11/3/16599816/washington-post-mcclatchy-miami-herald-ap-russian-propaganda-twitter

55 Kim Bredesen, *The press' immune defences are failing [Pressens immunforsvar svikter]* (1 December 2007). Le Monde Diplomatique Norway.

56 Ibid.

57 Alex Hern, Pamela Duncan & Ella Creamer, *Russian trolls' tweets cited in more than 100 UK news articles* (10 September 2018). Retrieved 16 April 20202 from The Guardian theguardian.com/media/2018/sep/10/russian-trolls-tweets-cited-in-more-than-100-uk-news-articles

58 Ståle Grut, *NRKbeta reveals: All major Norwegian media outlets have been duped by Russian troll accounts [NRKbeta avslører: Alle store norske medier har blitt lurt av russiske troll-kontoer]* (3 March 2020). Retrieved 30 March 2020 from NRKbeta nrkbeta.no/2020/03/03/nrkbeta-avslorer-alle-store-norske-medier-har-blitt-lurt-av-russiske-troll-kontoer

59 Ibid.

60 Nils Hanson, *Making Stories Ironclad & Bulletproof Line-by-Line* (presentation held 28 September 2019 at Global Investigative Journalism Conference 2019). Retrieved 10 December 2019 from Google Drive drive.google.com/file/d/1j0Rj5SCcJ9CwOZIhyswNqlPttSWgTaee/view

61 Erik Waatland, *NRK quoted fake Twitter-account: Wrote that Sylvy Listhaug (Progress party) would "return like an unexpected hurricane" [NRK siterte falsk Twitter-konto: Skrev at Sylvi Listhaug (Frp) ville "komme som en uventet orkan"]* (18 January 2019). Retrieved 5 September 2019 from Medier24 medier24.no/artikler/nrk-siterte-falsk-twitter-konto-skrev-at-sylvi-listhaug-frp-ville-komme-som-en-uventet-orkan/455821

62 Henrik Giæver, *NRK changed Greta Thunberg story after criticism: – Failed to explain the purpose of the story [NRK endret Greta Thunberg-sak etter kritikk: – Fikk ikke forklart målet med artikkelen]* (18 December 2019). Retrieved 11 January 2020 from Medier24 medier24.no/artikler/nrk-endret-greta-thunberg-sak-etter-kritikk-fikk-ikke-forklart-malet-med-artikkelen/481454

63 Ståle Grut, *Facebook and Twitter penalise China following influence campaign in Hong Kong [Facebook og Twitter straffer Kina etter påvirkningsoperasjon i Hongkong]* (20 August 2019). Retrieved 15 April 2020 from NRKbeta nrkbeta.no/2019/08/20/facebook-og-twitter-straffer-kina-etter-pavirkningsoperasjon-i-hongkong

64 Eirik Veum, *Attack on police in Hong Kong [Angriper polititjenestemenn i Hongkong]* (1 October 2019). Retrieved 15 October 2019 from NRK nrk.no/urix/angriper-polititjenestemenn-i-hongkong-1.14725923

65 Knight Center for Journalism in the Americas, *Module 1: Video 4 – A conversation with CNN disinformation reporter Donie O'Sullivan (Transcripts)* (2019). Retrieved 28 September 2019 from Knight Center for Journalism in the Americas journalismcourses.org/courses/VRFY0419/m1-4.pdf

66 Benjamin Strick, *How I Scrape and Analyse Twitter Networks: A Bolivian Info Op Case Study* (27 May 2020). Retrieved 27 May 2020 from <ben> benjaminstrick.com/how-i-scrape-and-analyse-twitter-networks

67 Gephi can be downloaded free of charge from gephi.org

68 A tool is "Reverse Analytics" from DNSlytics. You can also try using the Norwegian Broadcasting Corporation's code "UA-3413696" to see how it functions at dnslytics.com/reverse-analytics

69 Owen Mayer & Matthew C. Stamm, *Forensic Similarity for Digital Images* (24 June 2019). Retrieved 4 April 2020 from IEEE Transactions on Information Forensics and Security, 15, 1331–1346 doi.org/10.1109/TIFS.2019.2924552

70 Brian C. Hosler et al., *The Video Authentication and Camera Identification Database: A New Database for Video Forensics* (10 June 2019). Retrieved 16 April 2020 from IEEE Access, 7, 76937–76948 doi.org/10.1109/ACCESS.2019.2922145

71 Egil Fossum & Sidsel Meyer, *Er nå det så sikkert? [How can you be so sure?]* (2008). Cappelen Damm Akademisk.

72 Ibid.

73 Reuters, *Reuters toughens rules after altered photo affair* (21 January 2007). Retrieved 17 April 2020 from Reuters reuters.com/article/idUSL18678707

74 Lucinda Southern, *How Reuters is training reporters to spot 'deepfakes'* (26 March 2019). Retrieved 6 December 2019 Digiday digiday.com/media/reuters-created-a-deepfake-video-to-train-its-journalists-against-fake-news

75 Vasileios Mezaris et al., *Video Verification in the Fake News Era* (2019). Springer Nature

76 AFP, *#PrayforAmazonas: Thousands of people are sharing old pictures in posts about the Amazon rainforest fires* (22 August 2019). Retrieved 17 April 2020 from AFP Fact Check factcheck.afp.com/prayforamazonas-thousands-people-are-sharing-old-pictures-posts-about-amazon-rainforest-fires

77 Ole Alexander Saue, *– VG, TV 2 and NRK did not consider other perspectives at all – [VG, TV 2 og NRK tok overhovudet ikkje innover seg andre perspektiv]* (22 January 2019). Retrieved 12 January 2020 from Medier24 medier24.no/artikler/vg-tv-2-og-nrk-tok-overhovudet-ikkje-innover-seg-andre-perspektiv/456077

78 Washington Post Staff, *Editor's note related to Lincoln Memorial incident* (1 March 2019). Retrieved 6 December 2019 from The Washington Post washingtonpost.com/nation/2019/03/01/editors-note-related-lincoln-memorial-incident

79 Charlie Warzel, *The Fake Nancy Pelosi Video Hijacked Our Attention. Just as Intended.* (26 May 2019). Retrieved 9 December 2019 from The

New York Times nytimes.com/2019/05/26/opinion/nancy-pelosi-video-facebook.html

80 Harald S. Klungtveit, *Photographer fired for smoke tricks [Fotograf sparket for røyktriksing]* (7 August 2006). Retrieved 17 April 2020 from Dagbladet dagbladet.no/a/66239746

81 RTÉ news, *Croatian fire safety video lights up social media* (12 July 2018). Retrieved 17 April 2020 from RTÉ news rte.ie/news/newslens/2018/0712/978128-croatia-firefighters-safety-campaign
ABC News, "*WHEN DUTY CALLS: Croatian firefighters were desperate to see the end of their team's match against Russia in the World Cup quarterfinals–But when a call came into the station, they leapt into action. Croatia won seconds later.*" (11 July 2018). Retrieved 17 April 2020 from Wayback Machine web.archive.org/web/20180712025231/https://twitter.com/ABC/status/1017095024717295617

82 Anne-Marie Tomchak & Charlotte McDonald, *#BBCTrending: Syrian 'hero boy' video faked by Norwegian director* (14 November 2014). Retrieved 18 October 2019 from BBC News bbc.com/news/blogs-trending-30057401

83 Rushprint, *Norwegian Film Institute and Arts and Culture Norway apologise for Syria video [NFI og Kulturrådet beklager Syria-video]* (19 November 2014). Retrieved 18 October 2019 from Rushprint rushprint.no/rushes/nfi-og-kulturradet-beklager-syria-video

84 Nicole Bogart, *Video of snowboarder chased by bear was part of viral video 'social experiment'* (14 July 2016). Retrieved 17 April 2020 from Global News globalnews.ca/news/2824606/video-of-snowboarder-chased-by-bear-was-part-of-viral-video-social-experiment

85 Hilke Schellmann, *Deepfake Videos Are Getting Real and That's a Problem* (15 October 2018). Retrieved 24 October 2019 from Wall Street Journal wsj.com/video/series/moving-upstream/deepfake-videos-are-getting-real-and-that-a-problem/0C3815FB-82C7-4805-B902-31BEB0B4F146

86 Henry Ajder et al., *The State of Deepfakes: Landscape, Threats, and Impact* (September 2019). PDF retrieved 24 October 2019 from Deeptrace deeptracelabs.com/mapping-the-deepfake-landscape, p. 27.

87 Marius Arnesen, *Were all the vacation images you saw on social media this summer real? [Var alle feriebildene du så på sosiale medier i sommer ekte?]* (8 August 2019). Retrieved 17 April 2020 from NRKbeta nrkbeta.no/2019/08/08/var-alle-feriebildene-du-sa-pa-sosiale-medier-i-sommer-ekte

88 An example here is the website ThisPersonDoesNotExist.com, which through a "generative adversarial network" (GAN) generates fake human profile photos.

89 Nils Martin Silvola, *He has debated with press royalty Arne Jensen and is constantly in contact with journalists. However, neither his name nor his face exist [Han har debattert med pressetopp Arne Jensen og tar stadig kontakt med journalister. Men hverken navnet eller ansiktet hans*

eksisterer] (19 February 2020). Retrieved 17 April 2020 from Journalisten journalisten.no/ai-genererte-bilder-anonymitet-are-peder-johnsrud/han-har-debattert-med-pressetopp-arne-jensen-og-tar-stadig-kontakt-med-journalister-men-hverken-navnet-eller-ansiktet-hans-eksisterer/400421

90 Dan Stowell (one of the leaders of Machine Listening Lab at Queen Mary University of London, who does research on audio and machine listening), personal communication, 3 April 2020.
Truls Birkeland (music producer and senior engineer at the Department of Digital Policing and Innovation, Oslo Police District), personal communication, 7 April 2020.

91 BBC, *Adobe Voco 'Photoshop-for-voice' causes concern* (7 November 2016). Retrieved 26 October 2020 from BBC News bbc.com/news/technology-37899902

92 Nick Statt, *Podcast editor Descript adds new pro tier with access to its AI voice double feature* (28 July 2020). Retrieved 31 July 2020 from The Verge theverge.com/2020/7/28/21345063/descript-pro-ai-overdub-podcast-editor-subscription-service-features-pricing

93 Samantha Cole, *This AI-Generated Joe Rogan Voice Sounds So Real It's Scary* (17 May 2019). Retrieved 30 March 2020 from Motherboard vice.com/en_us/article/597yba/ai-generated-fake-joe-rogan-voice-dessa

94 Lorenzo Franceschi-Bicchierai, *Listen to This Deepfake Audio Impersonating a CEO in Brazen Fraud Attempt* (23 July 2020). Retrieved 5 September 2020 from Motherboard vice.com/en_us/article/pkyqvb/deepfake-audio-impersonating-ceo-fraud-attempt

95 ITV, *WhatsApp audio recording is slammed as fake news by Public Health England* (8 April 2020). Retrieved 31 July 2020 from ITV itv.com/news/central/2020-04-08/whatsapp-audio-recording-is-slammed-as-fake-news-by-public-health-england

96 Philippa Law (then social media and user-generated content editor at the Associated Press), personal communication, 3 April 2020.

97 Truls Birkeland (music producer and senior engineer at the Department of Digital Policing and Innovation, Oslo Police District), personal communication, 7 April 2020.

98 Catalin Grigoras, *Digital audio recording analysis: The Electric Network Frequency* (ENF) Criterion (2007). International Journal of Speech, Language and the Law.

99 Truls Birkeland (music producer and senior engineer at the Department of Digital Policing and Innovation, Oslo Police District), personal communication, 7 April 2020.

3 Verifying information

Introduction

Simply put, the process of verification entails testing the validity of claims. In the philosophy of science, verification is defined as arriving at an assessment of the degree of probability that something is true.[1] Using the term verification in a journalistic context requires some caution. In general, the term verification has some connotations connected to the natural sciences and their formal regime of hypothesis testing which do not necessarily adhere to knowledge production in the sociocultural domain associated with journalism.[2] As noted in Chapter 1, the journalistic epistemology is traditionally binary, on the basis of which a source is categorically deemed either trustworthy or untrustworthy. Steensen et al. regard this as a problem, as it does not adequately acknowledge how degrees of accuracy and reliability are dependent on sociocultural context and interpretation.[3] The result is an understanding of verification that pushes journalism into binary positions, forsaking the complexity required to produce truth-claims.[4]

This chapter is mostly concerned with the process of how journalists can best go about establishing the probability that something happened as depicted in a photo or video that surfaces online. The book refers to this process when using the term verification. The chapter will address in depth how images and videos from the Internet can be investigated, analysed and used in journalism once you are secure in the knowledge that the content is authentic, have revealed its relevant tendencies, and found that it contributes to the truthful depiction of an event.

As we will soon see, media content generated by the public, so-called user-generated content (UGC), is something every journalist will run into sooner or later. This content in particular requires

DOI: 10.4324/9781003449461-4

verification if it is to be used in journalism. Often it is a matter of news tips, or content published on social media. The media content can come from a local source – the city or country where you reside – or from a completely different place on the planet. Often it has substantial news value. By leveraging resources available on the Internet, it is possible to cross-check tips and media content using data on actual world events and situations. In this chapter, we will predominantly focus on verification of user-generated content related to news events, which constitutes a key portion of every journalist's digital daily life.

The layers of journalism

As mentioned in Chapter 1, we often need to use several and different types of sources to determine the facts of a past event.[5] This is necessary to confirm uncertain or controversial news elements, and to be able to present a richer and more nuanced image of the events in question.[6] In the textbook *News Writing and Reporting*, Melvin Mencher defines three layers of reporting that can help us understand and identify the different methods and what they entail.[7]

Layer 1 – source-originated: The first layer is *source-originated reporting*. In this case, the source is in the driver's seat. The journalist's job is to confirm that the source said what they said, but not to investigate the actual statements made by the source. In some cases reference is made to source materials, which according to Fossum and Meyers means that the journalist has "has done the work required to fulfil the conventions" because the source has been correctly cited.[8] Although a reference is cited for the claims, this does not automatically mean the claims are more credible. Layer 1 includes all constructed events and pseudo-events, such as happenings, press conferences, press releases, launches and other events for which the source's objective is to gain the attention of the public and the press corps – and often succeeds in doing just that.

Layer 2 – digging: Every journalist who gathers information beyond that which is presented by a source, and thereby digs deeper than Layer 1, is working at Layer 2. At this level, the journalist tells the story, in contrast to Layer 1, where it is the sources who are telling it.[9] It doesn't take much for a story to rise to this level. The criterion is that the journalist does the thinking about the issue and, on the basis of this, pulls in several different sources in order to establish what is true and false. It is the journalist who is in the driver's seat and not the source. Although not all stories at this level are equally thorough, it is the deep and thorough digging of *investigative reporting* that characterises Layer 2.

Layer 3 – analysis: Basically, we can say that Layer 1 refers to a source's account of something that took place. At Layer 2, the journalist presents his or her version of what took place. At the next level, the journalist's job is to explain why something happened. Layer 3 is characterised by the *analysis*, explanations of what took place and why, and explanations of causes and consequences.[10]

Figures and statistics in brief

The ability to navigate large quantities of numerical data and a critical approach to the presentation and analysis of registry data and other statistics are both important in the evaluation of digital sources. As discussed in Chapter 1, it is also important to be able to assess the quality of numerical data, its credibility, validity and the extent to which it is representative. Consequently, a certain amount of knowledge about statistics is required in the evaluation of digital sources. This can be the case when you must assess claims and source materials presented in graphs, graphics and computer-generated visualisations – or when as a journalist you are going to create this type of presentation yourself.

We have enormous access to figures and statistics today. This is particularly the case in Norway, where the transparency of public databanks is considerable. Statistics Norway is just one of many institutions that collect and present detailed data about Norwegian conditions and affairs, which journalists can use to evaluate sources or verify information. In this case it is also important for the journalist to investigate the sources of figures and graphs and not blindly trust the materials presented.

A method often used by actors who seek media coverage is to present findings from a survey they have commissioned along with their pitch for a story. Unfortunately, the public is frequently not given access to the objectives constituting the basis for the surveys. One example of this, which received a lot of attention in Norway, was when the Confederation of Norwegian Enterprise (NHO) presented a report in conjunction with the annual political gathering "Arendal Week" (*Arendalsuka*). A key piece of contextual information here is that this week-long event is used as a platform for launches by many different interest groups and companies. There is therefore cause to proceed with caution in coverage of this event so as to avoid excessive Layer 1 journalism.

The largest Norwegian daily *VG* headlined NHO's report at the top of its digital front page. The newspaper used words such as "alarm" and "warning lamps" in reference to the findings of a "shocking report" which revealed that young people do not feel it is important to live in a democracy. NHO's report cited figures from an existing study of attitudes and values done by World Value Survey (WVS). The original survey had not contained figures from Norway, so NHO had carried out its own survey using the same questions as WVS in order to be able to include Norway. Although the article in VG did not state as much, in culling answers to its questions, NHO had used a method that differed from the method used in the original survey.[11]

The NHO report and *VG*'s coverage were subjected to fact-checking on the part of both *Faktisk* and *Morgenbladet*. Both publications concluded that the claim was incorrect. In *Morgenbladet*, journalist Sigve Indregard wrote that "the figures and axes are misleading, but formally speaking correct". Both Indregard and *Faktisk* made reference to the use of the word "essential" in one of the questions regarding how important it is to live in a democracy. The word was used by NHO and repeated by *VG*. The word was not used in the original survey and was introduced by two political scientists who once wrote about the original study. No information about this was included in NHO's own report or in *VG*'s coverage of it.

Having knowledge about and the skills to understand and analyse figures and statistics is highly significant in the evaluation of digital sources. One solution is naturally for journalists to improve their expertise on figures, statistics and the presentation of these. As a journalist, you should also give the public access to any figures and supporting documents you reference or integrate into your story. The Danish journalist Ernst Poulsen proposes that the media should not cover surveys and public opinion polls at all, unless the public is given access to the supporting documentation or background materials.[12] In Norway, Indregard has called for a revision of the Ethical Code of Practice for the Norwegian Press, stipulating that statistics and other figures are to be included in publications.[13]

In the introductory book *Statistikk i praksis* ("Statistics in Practice"), sociologist Silje Bringsrud Fekjær writes about interpretive errors, stating that many of the most common of these are committed by journalists and the media.[14] It is not difficult to misinterpret statistics and make mistakes when translating figures into a story. As a journalist, it is therefore particularly important not to contribute to the misrepresentation of statistics or to create skewed presentations of results, because the potential audience for errors of this nature is huge. In her book, Fekjær points out six main pitfalls to look out for when interpreting statistics:

- *Confusing causality with statistical context:* Even though it is possible to prove that two phenomena occurred simultaneously, this does not demonstrate a connection between them. Other factors may be the actual cause.
- *Spuriousness*: Two phenomena appear to be connected, but actually it is a third, underlying variable that is the cause of both.
- *Reverse causality*: Sometimes a statistical connection between two phenomena says nothing about the cause. As an example, Fekjær offers the claim that those who eat breakfast are less depressed. The cause can also be the opposite: depressed individuals do not eat breakfast.
- *Selection*: Here Fekjær highlights in particular the media's use of surveys and polls. You should always evaluate whether the findings of a survey are due to the selection criteria defining the group of respondents, because a representative selection will provide a better basis for a survey.
- *Small distinctions:* Again journalists are spotlighted because minor distinctions and changes can be exaggerated. Statistics about rare phenomena can change abruptly, which in turn can lead to attention-grabbing headlines about occurrences that are not in fact particularly dramatic. By studying the results of a survey closely, subtle distinctions in the understanding of a situation can be discerned. Then the headline of a story must also be given nuance.
- *Vague presentation*: When you read about statistical surveys in the media, the journalist is serving as a filter for the information. Misinterpretations and misunderstandings can therefore lead to a vague rendering of the original source, which is obviously problematic. Media stories that present research can also create the impression that the research has produced more answers than the actual findings would suggest.

User-generated content

Images and videos captured by eyewitnesses using their own camera equipment are increasingly used by the media and have been a critical factor behind the success of large social media platforms. This is called *user-generated content*, often abbreviated as UGC.

Content of this nature is typically created by amateurs and not professionals.[15] For news-related purposes, this content has been of particular interest because the most powerful images from current events often come from eyewitnesses on the scene who are documenting the situation with their own cameras.[16] One of the first important events about which news organisations gained access to large amounts of user-generated content – amateur videos – was the tsunami in Southeast Asia just after Christmas in 2004.[17] Tourists in the affected nations used mobile phones and digital video cameras to document the enormous destruction in the wake of the tsunami that took around 230,000 human lives.[18]

Since then, due to technological development, high-resolution cameras and image sensors have become extremely widespread. You will find them on mobile phones, cars, doorbells, buildings, police uniforms – almost every type of device imaginable. Media scholar Sigurd Allern refers to user-generated content as a potential treasure trove of information and documentation for the news media.[19] But if user-generated content is to be used, verification is crucial. It is not solely necessary if the content is to be used in legal proceedings but also for use in journalism.[20] Verification must be done both with an eye to reporting credible information and to halting the dissemination of misleading or fabricated content.[21]

The challenges of verifying user-generated content are numerous. It is easy to be deceived here as well. The content itself, the media it comes from, and the sender can all contain problematic elements. No two stories are alike, and there is therefore no specific formula that will ensure a perfect and flawless result every time you verify media content. This is one of the key reasons why patience, creativity and improvisation are just as important in the verification process as the digital tools we have on hand for the investigation of information.[22] Such tools are continually evolving but will almost always have certain limitations. You must therefore often employ a variety of complementary tools that solve different types of problems. It should be specified here that the human brain is still the most important tool when it comes to verifying user-generated content.

News agencies such as Storyful work exclusively with finding user-generated content with news value on social media. Traditional agencies such as the Associated Press and Reuters have set up designated departments for this purpose. These news agencies perform the task of locating, verifying and distributing content from social media to their customers. The use of user-generated content in news production has now become so common that large corporations such as the BBC and CNN do this work in-house. In May 2023, the BBC greatly expanded this investment, presenting a team of around 60 journalists dubbed BBC Verify who "showcase the advanced editorial tools and techniques BBC News journalists are using to investigate, source and verify information, video, and images".[23] It is not common for all journalists to receive training in verification, even though knowledge about evaluating digital sources is actually required to work professionally with digital and web-based sources. Newsrooms will typically assign small groups of people to work exclusively on verifying and adapting user-generated content. *The Wall Street Journal* has created a resource group of more than 20 individuals whom the newspaper's journalists can contact when they need help determining whether or not a video has been manipulated.[24] For the individual journalist or a smaller news desk, assembling a similar group may seem impossible, but knowledge about verification is frequently and openly shared between colleagues on the Internet and social media, so it should be manageable for all journalists to stay more or less updated in this field by following talented specialists and their work.

It is not difficult to find exciting content on social media, but if you are unable to determine the where and when of the content's origin or whether the source is reliable, using it in editorial coverage is risky.[25] The industry organisation for digital journalists in the USA, the Online News Association, has produced a code of ethics for utilisation of user-generated content.[26] The code contains ten points, including standardised and practical advice for the use of such content, and regarding the dialogue with the public and sources. The points include being open with the public about how the content has been verified and proper crediting of those responsible for the content. The Irish journalist Malachy Browne describes well the opposite extremes on the scale of difficulty inherent to the process of verifying content and sources. At the one end of the scale, it can be as straightforward as comparing a video with Google Street View in order to identify a camera angle. At the opposite end, it can be as difficult as going through a video one frame at a time, and simultaneously analysing the sound waves and frequencies of the audio track to pinpoint details.[27] When verification becomes this advanced, the process approaches highly specialised police and intelligence work which is described in further detail in Chapter 4. In any event, user-generated content should always be verified before it is used in journalism.

The verification process

How should you proceed when you have found something of interest on the Internet that you want to use editorially? All the steps you must take to verify the origin of media content found on the Internet are outlined below. The process is adapted to include visual content such as images and videos. The term "images" will be used, although the steps will for the most part also apply to videos. The search options for video content are extremely limited, and the solution is often therefore to use screenshots from the video in question and in this way search for clues in the same way you would with images.

The verification process may seem elaborate, but it is necessary in order to ensure that content can be published in a responsible manner in the media. The initial steps can quickly disclose the origin of content and it will therefore not always be necessary to do all of the steps for all types of content. A general rule of thumb for the entire process is to take notes, save screenshots and bookmark the website links you encounter along the way. You must make sure to maintain an overview of the process so you can go back and double-check details. If you have good notes and clearly organised documentation to rely on, you will avoid frustration and save time, and be better equipped when you present your findings to colleagues or your audience.

1 News monitoring, discovery and search

The editorial task of verification starts with a tip, a discovery or the active gathering of media content related to news events. Large news agencies are often a good source of tips and provide quick access to content. To find niche stories or "softer" news from your own coverage region more quickly, social media can offer contact with potentially solid sources. Large news agencies have, as stated, set up their own desks in such a way as to enable them to find stories quickly through social media, and there is a lot to be learned from their methods.

To find information about an ongoing incident quickly, the social media-focused news agency Storyful started creating hundreds of Twitter lists based on different themes and locations. They gathered user accounts managed by people in conflict zones such as Syria, or who frequently published updates about the country. The method provided them with a list of fresh updates from a long series of relevant locations and communities. This made it easier to gain an overview if something happened in a conflict region or newsworthy events occurred in a range of categories, such as FIFA, the auto industry or the weather. With time, these lists were developed or combined with systems of their own design, which gather user accounts from a variety of social media and will alert a news desk of events as they occur.[28]

Several platforms, such as Samdesk, Geofeedia and Dataminr, sell tools that perform this task to news desks, the public authorities and other organisations. By monitoring dramatic key terms (such as "murder", "explosion", "kidnapping" etc.) in both English and local languages, alerts can be generated in their systems in response to events. Samdesk has among other strategies linked the social media user accounts of reputable agents to geographic location. This means they can quickly locate official and reliable sources if their automatic surveillance systems pick up content or activity related to key terms that can be of interest to journalists.

There are several ways of finding content from a specific location, even though only a small portion of the information published on social networks actually includes geolocation data.[29] Let's say you are searching for content about a concert at a popular venue in London. Services such as Geofeedia will enable you to highlight an area around the venue and intercept published content with geolocation data from around the concert. Because only a small portion of published content contains geolocation data, you will usually have to navigate using key terms, user tags or hashtags to find more.

One of the advantages of being a local journalist in this phase is the language barrier. The greater your mastery of a language, the more jargon, dialects and slang you can use in your searches. Here it is important to think like a user who shares content and search for words or hashtags that this person would have used.

2 The content

When you find content online and on social media, there are several steps you should take to ensure secure use of that content in journalism. There are a number of different guides available that specify the questions you should ask when you come across documentation of events from eyewitnesses. Essentially, this process entails finding the original, determining who shared it, their location, when they were there and why they shared what they did. These guides also warn about the pitfalls and errors that can arise in the verification process.[30] It all starts with going to the source.

2.1 Find the first share (provenance)

When you find interesting content on the Internet, you should never assume that what you are looking at is the original. Because it is so easy to copy, download and upload data on the Internet, content can spread quickly across websites and (social) media. The key is therefore to find the source of the dissemination, in other words, the first time an image or video was shared on the Internet. This will give you the best basis for making contact with the first person to upload content or make a claim, which is often necessary in order to determine whether the content is authentic and, where relevant, to clear the content for editorial use. It is important to work with the original source, because all the metadata about the origin and uploading time can otherwise be misleading.

A good place to start evaluating media content is to look at image quality. Original content will usually be high resolution, good quality and without watermarks. Copied content often presents the opposite: it is low resolution, of poor quality and has perhaps one or more watermarks. If an image is shared through a messaging app and subsequently makes its way to Reddit and from there to Facebook, every time it is uploaded or downloaded the quality is diminished. This is because most social media platforms compress media content to facilitate effective distribution and so it occupies less space in their data centres. Some also claim it is done to ensure the privacy of its users. This makes the task of tracking down sources difficult, because all the original metadata is removed from the content when it is uploaded onto social media.[31]

Those who upload others' content are typically and erroneously presumed to be the source. Imagine a scenario in India, as an example in which content initially appears on a messaging app, such as

WhatsApp; or in the case of Iran, on Telegram, a popular app there. It will often take hours or even days for content to spread to social media platforms that are more open and accessible for Western citizens and journalists. But the origin is not necessarily the Facebook page where you first saw the video. If the text and audio are in a foreign language, you should enlist somebody's help to produce a precise translation. Perhaps there is someone who works at the news desk or in your company who can provide assistance. A list specifying staff members' language proficiency at a news desk can be a valuable resource for the quick resolution of such a problem. Otherwise, look for someone in your local community, journalist colleagues in other countries or professional translators who can help you.

Copies represent a particular challenge in the context of ongoing news events, especially on and from messaging apps such as WhatsApp, Telegram, and Snapchat. Although someone has shared an image or video content on social media, it could be that the content actually comes from a wholly different online source. There are also user accounts that gather and quickly publish eyewitness videos on the heels of an event, in hopes of generating traffic and revenues. Videos of this nature are called *scrapes*. An example of a scape would be the video from the horrific massacre in Christchurch, New Zealand which was broadcast live on Facebook. The footage was not immediately taken down by Facebook and was therefore viewed many times. In the course of the first 24 hours after the video was published, Facebook removed 1.5 million versions of the video that others had attempted to upload.[32]

2.2 Find the original source

When you have found the first known share, a reverse image search is a good place to start digging for the original source. On a number of search engines such as TinEye, Bing, Yandex and Google, you can upload an image and search for formerly posted versions on the Internet. The method is called "reverse image search". Handy browser add-ons such as RevEye will allow you to right-click an image and carry out visual searches on several search engines simultaneously. The different search engines that currently exist are good at different things (objects, faces, places, different resolutions), so it pays to carry out searches using several.[33] You can also add key words to image searches to improve the search's precision. To do a more specific search for a place, a room, a thing or the surroundings in an image, you can use an editing program such as Photoshop to blur other objects or people in the image. The search engine will then focus on the sharp elements in the image.[34]

To do searches on video content, you can upload screenshots from the video and do image searches. Try using the first image that appears in the video or a screenshot of particular interest from the documented event. Browser add-ons such as Video Screenshot and InVID simplify the process of retrieving stills with the original resolution intact from different video services, and the latter have several tools that can be used to evaluate content authenticity. If the material is presented as stemming from a given event, such as a demonstration, it makes sense to ascertain whether the event has actually taken place through use of other sources. Introducing a date restriction is one helpful method. In this way you can search exclusively for results up until a given date and thereby suppress copies of content published after an event became extremely popular and began dominating search engine results. It is useful to make a note of as much contextual information as possible in the course of the verification process, because this will often come in handy down the road. What happened before or after the featured content was documented? Always remember to take notes and save documentation during the verification process.

When you have reached the point in the process where you can establish that the content is genuine and the source is real, it may feel as if you have finished the job. You should nonetheless search for additional sources. Once you have verified a piece of content, you can use the information gathered through this task to help you track down other sources. This work can often proceed quite quickly, because you already know a lot about the situation and the content. Try to find out whether others were present. Maybe somebody else has documented what took place after the fact? Using the search terms you have disclosed or contacts on the scene, you can track down additional content to strengthen and inform your coverage.

If you have gained access to the original file, you will then also have access to metadata that tells you more about the content. There are both applications and websites available which will enable you to upload media content and read Exif information and other data. Exif stands for "exchangeable image file format" and is a standard for storing detailed data about media content, which gives you the chance to peek behind the curtain, as it were. The data typically shows the type of camera used to create the content, the manufacturer, the focal

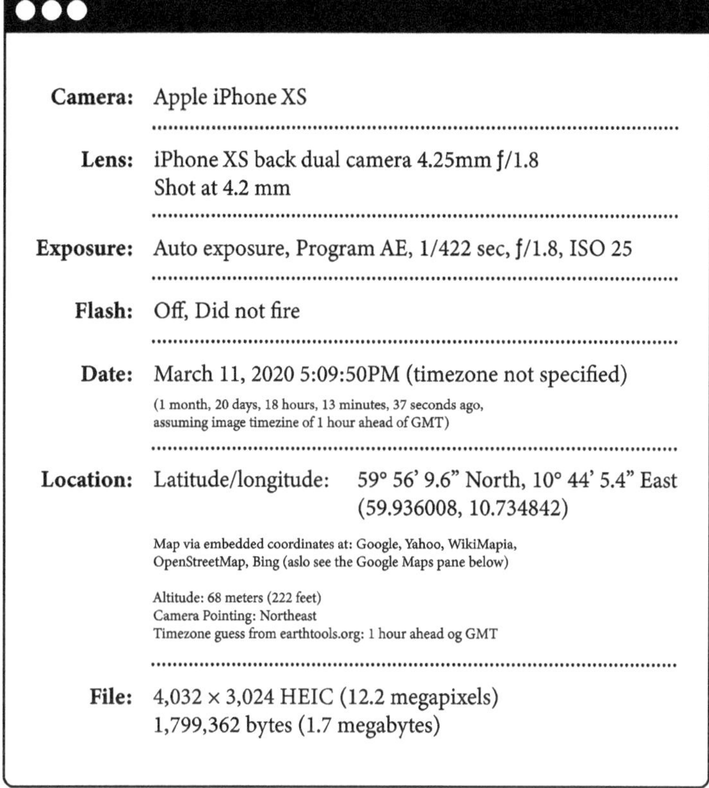

Figure 3.1 Some of the metadata available on a photo taken with a cell phone retrieved via the web-based software Jeffrey's Exif Viewer.

length of the lens, GPS data and when the file was created. The list of information can be long, but be aware that it is relatively simple to both edit and remove this information.

2.3 Geolocation

The precise location of where the video or photo was captured should then be determined. This is commonly referred to as geolocation. Map services such as Google Earth and Bing Maps are useful tools for this task because they contain aerial images of the entire planet. Satellite imagery is also available from a number of platforms. Many websites offer sharp aerial images from local regions. A number of regions have also been meticulously documented at the ground level by various stakeholders and at different times. Google Street View is one of these.

Scrutinise the images carefully for visual hints such as buildings, billboards or street signs in the image or video and try to pinpoint the location on the map. This can be a difficult exercise but becomes easier with practice and if you have some help to begin with. The geography game GeoGuessr is one way of practising geolocation skills. Geolocation is the most important basic skill required in the task of verifying content. A study of people who carried out geolocation identified the elements that were particularly useful in the work of solving geolocation tasks.[35] Architecture, language, typeface, traffic rules, the position of the sun, and animals were predominantly used to identify the continent or nation in which images were taken. Signs on buildings, roads, shops and landmarks provide more precise details about the city or street featured in an image but require tools such as search engines. Remember that practice makes perfect and all the information you accumulate will be useful in the future.

When a video of a police raid in the Netherlands targeting a suspect for three killings on a streetcar in Utrecht in 2019 appeared on the Internet, Norwegian journalist Angelica Hagen began the task of verifying the images. She drove around the neighbourhood in question and compared the buildings in the video with the buildings she saw from the car – which can also be done digitally on Google Street View and other similar type services. Using this strategy, Hagen's news outlet was the first to identify the location in question.[36]

2.4 Establish the date and time

The next step is to establish the date and time of the source material. Archival images are commonly used to illustrate an ongoing or alleged event, even though the image may have nothing to do with the event in question. A classic example here is how more or less iconic photos from a specific demonstration are used to illustrate another. When you find content on social media, it is also important to remember that the upload date and time associated with the content will usually be later than the actual moment of documentation or capture. A few minutes or hours may pass from the time a video is shot until the content is uploaded and posted. Different social media and websites also display the date and time in different ways, so the format of the metadata can differ, and this must be factored into your assessment.

It is also possible to determine the date and time of an image even though you do not have access to metadata or other information about the image. The method for establishing the date and time of media content without the use of metadata is called *chronolocation*.[37] There are two main methods used to establish the time frame for a photo or video:

- the length of shadows;
- timekeeping devices in the image.

Scouring images for timekeeping devices such as a wristwatch, a clock on a church tower, or a mobile phone is the simplest method for establishing the time. If a car dashboard is visible, the hour and temperature may be indicated. Former BBC journalist Benjamin Strick proposes more creative solutions: if a petrol station can be seen in the background, the price of petrol may be clearly advertised and this can provide information about when the photo was taken. Historical fuel prices can be found on a national database. The price in the photo can be cross-referenced against this or other data from the petrol station. The colour of foliage can indicate whether the photo was taken in the spring or the autumn. Wolfram Alpha also offers historical weather data that can be an indication of the temperature or whether the sky was actually overcast at the moment you estimate the photo was taken.

The second method involves calculating the length of the shadows in images, similar to the way shadows are measured on a sundial to indicate the time. Since the orbit and rotation of the earth are predictable, the sun will be in a specific position at any given day and time.[38] By obtaining four variables, it can be possible to identify the time and date an image was captured.[39] These are:

1. Height: How tall is the object or person in the image casting a shadow?
2. Length: How long is the shadow?
3. Altitude/zenith: What is the sun's position above the horizon?
4. Azimuth: From what direction is the sun shining?

If you have found the location on the map, you can use tools such as SunCalc, which will show the date and time when the shadows would have been at this angle and length.[40]

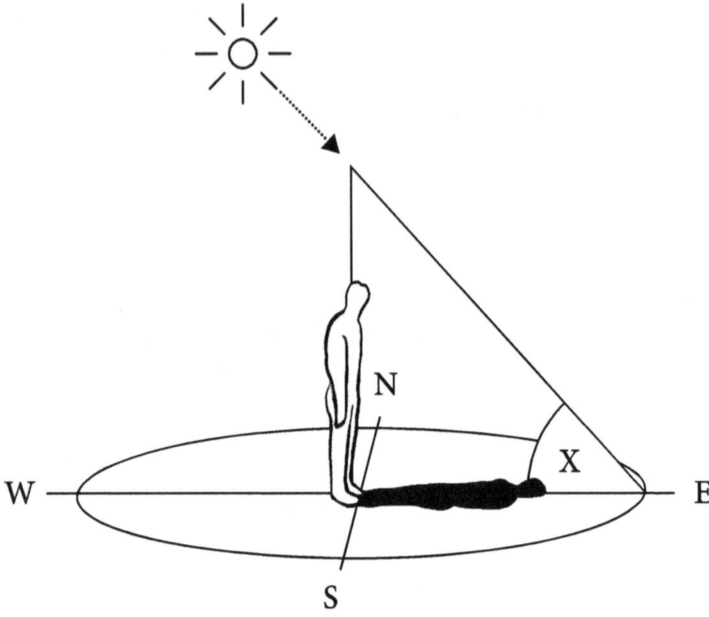

Figure 3.2 The shadow of a human being can provide information about when a photo was taken.

2.5 Motivation

On this point, the digital methods intersect solidly with the methods traditionally used in journalism and source criticism. It is important to understand the source's motivation for sharing the content. It can be a matter of an eyewitness who happened to be present when an event occurred, an activist interested in documenting something specific, or personnel from the emergency services who arrived on the scene after an accident occurred.

Before you start this process, it can be a good idea to follow your instincts. Consider the likelihood that the person who shared the content was actually on the scene when the event occurred. Would this person have shared this particular image or video of the events?

3 The sender

Ideally, you will begin the process of investigating the sender in conjunction with your investigations of the content. Because the origin of the content and the sender can be completely different, this endeavour can easily turn into two parallel and possibly divergent processes. Let us take a closer look at how you can investigate and work with the content's sender.

3.1 Analyse the sender's user account and social media history

There is always cause to be sceptical about a user account that has been recently set up. One of the most difficult things to falsify on social media is a long history. Although a user account is apparently represented on different social media platforms and a website, these may have been set up a short time ago, precisely to make it seem as if an actual human being is behind them and/or has a well-established internet presence. On the website you can see when the domain was registered (this can be done using a *whois*-protocol query), but simultaneously, you must remember that it is easier to backdate content published on one's own website, because the information there can be edited at any time. Again network reading is useful: What do other sources have to say about this user account or website? Is the page linked to or cited by any credible stakeholders? Has the page existed in its current form for a long time? Are the archived versions of the same domain similar?

On social media, a large discrepancy between the number of followers and the number a user account is following can be an indication that something is off. It is also possible to do a reverse image search on the profile photos of suspicious profiles, because user accounts passing themselves off as authentic often steal images or the identities of unsuspecting individuals to appear genuine. Although we are looking at the credibility of one user account, the key to evaluating digital sources lies in analysing the user account network.[41] As stated in the section "Image and video manipulation" (Chapter 2), it can be useful to study the user's profile photo closely to determine whether the photo itself may have been computer-generated. This technique produces a unique profile photo that is difficult to track, and the use of such images is becoming more prevalent.

3.2 Establish contact

If you plan to use the content in journalism, you should make contact with the person who has shared the content. The disadvantage of this is that it takes time. The advantage is clearly that you thereby diminish the risk of incorrect reporting. You should ideally use alternative communication channels when making contact, as opposed to through the platform where you initially discovered the content. It may be wise to encrypt information sent to the contact on the alternative channel. Direct communication will help to reveal more information about the individual behind the user account: is it a random eyewitness, an automated user account, or someone who is trying to deceive you? At the same time, you avoid disclosing to other journalists that you have a dialogue with the source, in the event you want to keep this information confidential.

The quickest and simplest means of achieving a dialogue with such a source is over the phone. If you speak with someone on the telephone, this alone is an indication of the source's credibility. If the person in question does not want to speak with you or is reluctant to share details, this can be a sign that the source is unreliable.[42] To avoid spreading disinformation, one option is to establish guidelines stipulating that media content will only be used editorially if the journalist has spoken with the source over the phone.[43]

3.3 Ask questions

Once contact with the original source is established, your conduct in interaction with the source should provide assurance that they are in safe hands. Eyewitnesses may have just experienced something traumatic, may still be in danger, or may be in an exigent or difficult situation. According to First Draft, in the context of ongoing events there are at least five points you should clarify with a source who has shared user-generated content:[44]

1. Ask how they are doing. Although the source may be safe in a physical sense, they may be in a state of shock or affected by stress.
2. Be clear about what news outlet or organisation you represent.
3. Explain how you found them and the content they have shared on social media. They may think they have shared something privately, or at least not with a journalist working for a news organisation.
4. Explain how you hope this content can strengthen or substantiate the story you are writing.
5. Give them your professional email address and the phone number for the news desk. Then the source can both reach you if necessary and rest secure in the knowledge that you actually are who you say you are. Trust is a two-way street.

When this has been done, the time has come to gather further information about the content. When was the photo taken? Can the source confirm the location of where the video was made? Did the source film it themselves? Does the source have other video clips or images from the situation, either before or after, that they would be willing to send you? Questions of this nature should be asked either through the channel of your initial contact or through an alternative channel, such as over the phone. If you get hold of the original files and any other content the source might possess, this will also assist you in the task of verification.

If you are in contact with a source on a messaging app, this is an effective file-sharing channel. As with most social media, the metadata is removed when photos are sent on messaging apps, and they are also compressed to occupy less space. One trick for acquiring as much information as possible is to ask the source to send media content as a file or a document on a messaging app. If you choose to send a photo as a "document" on WhatsApp, the photo and video will not be compressed and the metadata will be preserved. To do this on an iPhone you must first find the photo/video, tap on the share icon and choose "Save to Files". You can then send media content as a file on messaging apps. This enables you to send the original file with the metadata intact.[45]

3.4 Acquire consent for use and credit the source

A quick search using phrases like "*use your video*" on Twitter will unearth a number of journalists who take shortcuts and gather content without necessarily speaking on the phone with the person who shared the content. This of course accelerates the process but skips a number of steps they should have taken to strengthen the credibility of the information they are reporting. In the case of ongoing news events, if someone has shared a video or photo, the number of queries they receive can be substantial. If the number of queries from journalists requesting permission to use a video or an image "for free, on all our platforms in all perpetuity" becomes overwhelming, this can trigger a negative reaction on the part of both eyewitnesses and the public in general. It can therefore be useful to search for alternatives and see if others have shared videos or photos from the event whom you might contact instead. Eyewitnesses seldom have objections to sharing photos or videos. In my experience, they seldom have ambitions of any financial gain and would like to share what they have just experienced with a large audience.

To protect themselves, some journalists use different approaches to acquire the rights for use of content. Some ask to use the content in exchange for attribution, while others want "unlimited use on all our platforms" etc. A number of news agencies, such as Eurovision News Exchange and Storyful, have produced a document that they link to requests when collecting material from social media. In queries to eyewitnesses on social media, journalists from these agencies include links to pages on their own website that stipulate conditions.[46] This may seem complicated and somewhat over the top, but it can help prevent conflicts after the fact.

4 Confirm your story's consistency

If this is not already clear, at this point you should ensure the consistency of the source and the content. You should be able to identify the origin of the content and the process by which it came into your possession.

5 Editorial approval

Subsequently, you must clear use of the content in your editorial chain of command. Will your editor vouch for the publication of the content? Is the presentation in accordance with the journalistic code of ethics? An extremely important issue to think about before publishing user-generated content is whether it is sufficiently anonymised.

6 Publication and broadcasting

When you have gone through and carried out all the above steps, you will have a solid foundation for presenting the content to your audience. Be sure to include good, precise references for your sources, and above all give credit to the person responsible for the content. The user account name and the website where the content was shared can also be included in the credit. It is good practice to include a link to the content so the public can easily access the original source.

Verification and mental health

A fundamental issue for journalists and others working with the verification of user-generated content is how to avoid being affected by exposure to that content. Trawling the Internet for images from war zones, disasters or other dramatic events can be a strain and can even put your mental health at risk. A number of news stories have illuminated the trauma experienced by the moderators of large platforms, induced by long-term exposure to offensive and violent content.[47] Journalist Casey Newton reported that content moderators working for YouTube had to sign a release form acknowledging that they were aware that they could develop post-traumatic stress disorder (PTSD).[48] At the same time Facebook agreed to a settlement with more than 10,000 moderators, several of whom had developed PTSD on the job.[49]

When as a journalist you are working closely with this type of content, you may feel surrounded, because images are constantly popping up on your phone and on different screens in the newsroom. Research shows that some journalists who are frequently exposed to violent media content may experience a negative reaction.[50] In a study of about 250 journalists, almost half stated that watching disturbing user-generated content had been detrimental to their personal lives.[51] The after-effects included a grim view of the world, flashbacks, nightmares, stress and feelings of isolation. Newsrooms should therefore take precautions and monitor journalists who are exposed to this type of user-generated content. Former editor of user-generated content at the Associated Press, Fergus Bell, offers the following advice:[52]

- Limit individual journalists' exposure. Rotate the journalists who are required to view this type of content.
- If there is reasonable cause to assume the content will not be used, do not review it.
- Cover parts of the screen with your hand or sticky notes.
- It is a good idea to take frequent breaks and do something uplifting. Some people cope by checking in on cat blogs or thinking happy thoughts during a verification session.
- Cool off afterwards. Try to get the impressions out of your system.
- Have a colleague standing by who is aware that you are viewing this type of content and who can look for signs that you are suffering adverse effects.
- Make sure to have the option of saying "that is enough for now", without having to worry about what others might think.
- Small news desks that do not have experience with serious fieldwork and debriefing can run into more difficulties than large desks that have experience and a support system in place.

- Introduce best practice and procedures for verification as soon as possible; a problem may quickly develop if you do not take steps at an early stage.

In summary, you must be certain about content from the Internet before you can use it in journalism. This means that you must verify the content but also evaluate the source that has shared the content. The editorial process of verification can appear quite complex when all the above steps are listed at the same time, as in the illustration below inspired by the work of Fergus Bell.[53] Yet it is not all that difficult once it has become a habitual aspect of your journalistic practice. This overview of the verification process in the form of a flowchart is basically a systematic rendering of common sense.

Verification resources

First Draft News was an independent non-profit organisation founded by Claire Wardle and others. The organisation was one of the foremost providers of information about inaccurate digital content and practical tips and training for journalists. They published videos, handbooks and other materials that remain useful for all journalists working with verification. Introductory courses such as "Quick start to verifying online media" are recommended. The website page for practical tools called "Verification toolbox" is a good place for beginners to start working with verification:

firstdraftnews.org

Different verification tools are available and you should stay updated about such tools. Lists of digital tools and services have an unfortunate tendency to become quickly outdated, but the journalist Craig Silverman has worked with the verification of content for many years and he is unlikely to be hanging up his hat any time soon. In the following document and newsletter, Silverman compiles helpful verification and digital investigation tools:

bit.ly/verificationtoolsandtips
digitalinvestigations.substack.com

The verification handbooks published in 2014, 2015 and 2020, respectively, were created by Silverman and some of the best-known experts in the field. The books are a comprehensive resource containing international cases and are available in several languages. The book from 2014 is predominantly about verification of content from news events, and in 2015 an edition devoted to investigative journalism was published. The book from 2020 focuses on disinformation and media manipulation. All the books are available free of charge:

Verification: verificationhandbook.com
Investigative journalism: verificationhandbook.com/book2
Manipulation: datajournalism.com/read/handbook/verification-3

Editorial guidelines for user-generated content should be established at every news desk. Take a look at the guidelines from the BBC for inspiration:

bbc.com/editorialguidelines/guidance/user-generated-contributions

Practice makes perfect! Follow @quiztime on Twitter, where several days a week a new photo is posted for the purpose of identifying its geographical location. You can solve geolocation riddles with other interested individuals and receive tips on experts who can be queried for advice and assistance.

twitter.com/quiztime

Questions for reflection and exercises

- Find the last news story you read that cited the results of a survey. How difficult is it to track down the supporting documents?
- Take a look at the front page of some large and small news sites. How much of the content is user-generated?
- Read some of the captions accompanying user-generated content. Are the sources cited in detail beyond the classic tag "Photo: Social Media"? Is information provided about whether the platform acquired permission to use the photo? Does the medium have official guidelines for use of such content?
- Review the Exif data from an image you have taken using a photo program or web-based service such as Jeffrey's Exif Viewer. How

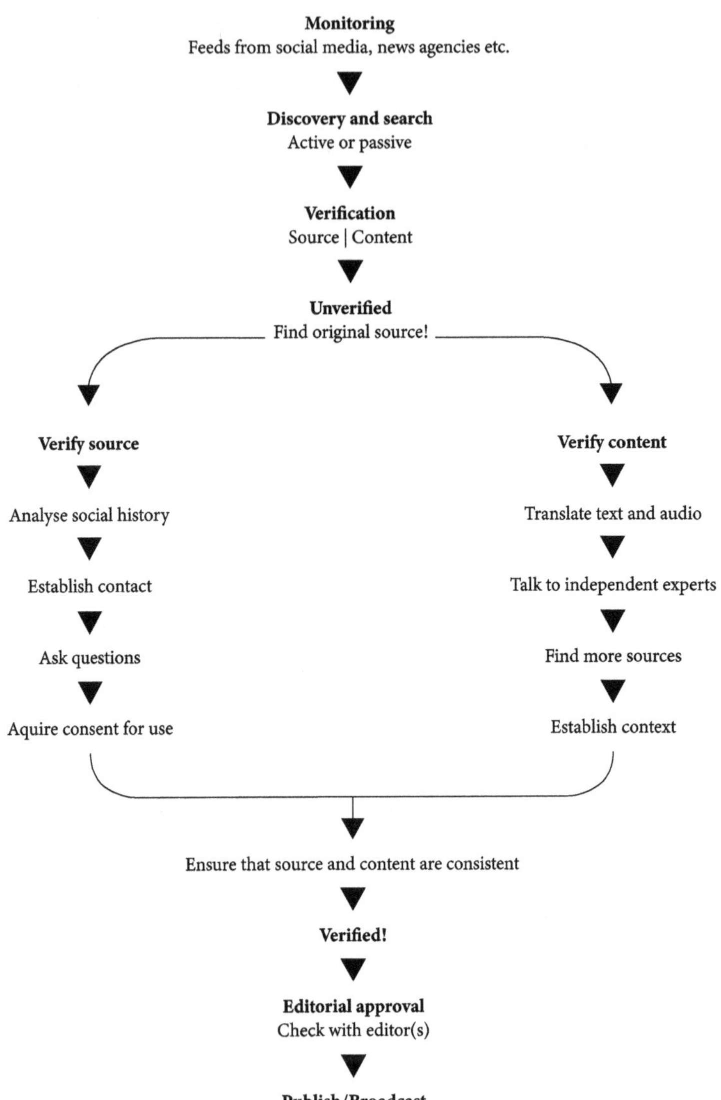

Figure 3.3 A workflow chart for verification at news desks, inspired by the work of Fergus Bell.

many data points can you access? Were there any you were not aware had been saved?

- Find a photo containing shadows. Can you determine when the photograph was taken? If you use an original file, the answer will most likely be found in the metadata.

Notes

1 Torsten Thurén, *Theory of Science for Beginners [Vitenskapsteori for nybegynnere]* (2009). Gyldendal Akademisk, p. 31.
2 Steen Steensen et al, *Journalism and Source Criticism. Revised Approaches to Assessing Truth-Claims* (2022). Journalism Studies, 0(0), 1–19. doi.org/10.1080/1461670X.2022.2140446
3 Ibid.
4 Ibid.
5 Egil Fossum & Sidsel Meyer, *Er nå det så sikkert? [How can you be so sure?]* (2008). Cappelen Damm Akademisk, p. 91.
6 Ibid.
7 Melvin Mencher, *Melvin Mencher's News Reporting and Writing*. 12th edition (2011). McGraw-Hill.
8 Egil Fossum & Sidsel Meyer, *Er nå det så sikkert? [How can you be so sure?]* (2008). Cappelen Damm Akademisk, p. 82.
9 Ibid, p. 88.
10 Melvin Mencher, *Melvin Mencher's News Reporting and Writing*. 12th edition (2011). McGraw-Hill.
11 Sigve Indregard, *No, NHO, youth do not think democracy is unimportant [Nei, NHO, ungdom mener ikke at demokrati er uviktig]* (22 August 2018). Retrieved 2 April 2020 from Morgenbladet morgenbladet.no/aktuelt/2018/08/nei-ungdom-mener-ikke-demokrati-er-uviktig-skriver-sigve-indregard
12 Ernst Poulsen, "*We need a new dogma in Danish journalism: 'We do not mention surveys and opinion polls without giving the readers access (links) to the documentation / background material.'" [Vi skal have et nyt dogme i dansk journalistik: "Vi omtaler ikke undersøgelser og meningsmålinger uden at give læserne adgang (links) til dokumentationen / baggrundsmateriale. "]* (14 November 2019). Retrieved 2 April 2020 from Twitter twitter.com/ernstpoulsen/status/1194918858219511809
13 Sigve Indregard, *Real responses to fake news [Ekte grep mot falske nyheter]* (24 February 2020). Retrieved 2 April 2020 from Indregard indregard.no/2020/02/ekte-grep-mot-falske-nyheter
14 Silje Bringsrud Fekjær, *Statistics in Practice [Statistikk i praksis]* (2016). Gyldendal Akademisk.
15 Petter Bae Brandtzæg & Marika Lüders, *eCitizen 2.0 – The ordinary citizen as a supplier of public information [eBorger 2.0 – Den alminnelige*

borger som leverandør av offentlig informasjon] (2008). Retrieved 26 May 2020 from Regjeringen regjeringen.no/globalassets/upload/fad/vedlegg/ikt-politikk/e_borger_20.pdf

16 Claire Wardle, *A journalist's guide to working with social sources* (September 2016). Retrieved 10 September 2019 from First Draft firstdraftnews.org/wp-content/uploads/2016/09/First-Draft-A-Journalists-Guide-To-Approaching-Social-Sources.pdf, p. 56.

17 Sam Dubberley, Alexa Koenig & Daragh Murray, *Digital Witness* (2020). Oxford University Press, p. 5.

18 Ellen Omland, Ingunn Andersen & Glen Imrie, *The tsunami ten years after: This is what you need to know [Tsunamien ti år etter: Dette trenger du å vite]* (20 December 2014). Retrieved 13 April 2020 from NRK nrk.no/urix/xl/tsunamien-ti-ar-etter_-dette-trenger-du-a-vite-1.12111187

19 Sigurd Allern, *Journalism and source critical analysis [Journalistikk og kildekritisk analyse]* (2015). Cappelen Damm Akademisk, p. 47.

20 Petter Bae Brandtzæg et al., *Emerging Journalistic Verification Practices Concerning Social Media* (2016). Journalism Practice, 10(3), 323–342 doi.org/10.1080/17512786.2015.1020331

21 Aric Toler in Sam Dubberley, Alexa Koenig & Daragh Murray, *Digital Witness* (2020). Oxford University Press, p. 186.

22 Ibid.

23 Bron Maher, *BBC unveils Verify team of 60 journalists it says will be 'transparency in action'* (17 May 2023). Retrieved 7 August 2023 from Press Gazette pressgazette.co.uk/news/bbc-verify

24 Lucinda Southern, "*A perfect storm*"*: The Wall Street Journal has 21 people detecting 'deepfakes'* (1 July 2019). Retrieved 12 September 2019 from Digiday digiday.com/media/the-wall-street-journal-has-21-people-detecting-deepfakes

25 Claire Wardle said this in the MOOC "*Navigating Misinformation: How to identify and verify what you see on the web*" under the direction of The Knight Center for Journalism in the Americas at the University of Texas.

26 The code of ethics is titled "*ONA Social Newsgathering Ethics Code*" and is available on ONA's website. Retrieved 19 September 2019 from Online News Association journalists.org/tools/social-newsgathering

27 Malachy Browne, *Reporting on Las Vegas, Pixel by Pixel* (23 October 2017). Retrieved 16 April 2020 from The New York Times nytimes.com/2017/10/23/insider/reporting-on-las-vegas-pixel-by-pixel.html

28 Abigail Edge, *5 tools Storyful recommends for social media monitoring* (12 November 2014). Retrieved 19 September 2019 from Journalism.co.uk journalism.co.uk/news/5-tools-storyful-recommends-for-social-media-monitoring-and-verification/s2/a563015

29 Neither Twitter nor Instagram wish to provide more recent figures for this book. We do know that for 2012, the figure was 2% for Twitter and between 15% and 25% for Instagram in 2013.

Ian Cairns, *Get More Twitter Geodata With Our New Profile Geo Enrichment* (22 August 2013). Retrieved 1 November 2019 from GNIP Company Blog (archived at Wayback Machine) web.archive.org/web/20130827220520/http://blog.gnip.com:80/twitter-geo-data-enrichment
Jenna Wortham, *Instagram Refreshes App by Including Photo Maps* (16 August 2012). Retrieved 23 October 2019 from New York Times Bits Blog bits.blogs.nytimes.com/2012/08/16/instagram-refreshes-app-include-photo-maps

30 A number of guides are available that describe these processes in detail. The steps presented in this book are based on the guide presented by Claire Wardle and First Draft: Claire Wardle, *A journalist's guide to working with social sources* (September 2016). Retrieved 10 September 2019 from First Draft firstdraftnews.org/wp-content/uploads/2016/09/160914_FirstDraft_WhitePaper_Digital.pdf

31 Matthew Stamm is a researcher in information forensics, and made this statement during the panel discussion "*Easy to Fool? Journalism in the Age of Deepfakes*" at the conference South by Southwest in 2019. An audio recording is available at: soundcloud.com/officialsxsw/sxsw-2019-easy-to-fool-journalism-in-the-age-of-deepfakes

32 Chris Sonderby, *Update on New Zealand* (18 March 2019). Retrieved 1 November 2019 from Facebook Newsroom newsroom.fb.com/news/2019/03/update-on-new-zealand

33 Ryan Weaver, *A Brief Comparison of Reverse Image Searching Platforms* (10 September 2019). Retrieved 18 November 2019 from Domaintools domaintools.com/resources/blog/a-brief-comparison-of-reverse-image-searching-platforms

34 Aric Toler, *"So, what we need to do is reverse search the full image to feed as many pixels as possible into the algorithm, but taking out the person so it doesn't just focus on finding other women standing in front of things. I use Snagit to blur her out for this image"* (16 December 2019). Retrieved 17 December 2019 from Twitter twitter.com/AricToler/status/1206680425134985221

35 Sneha Mehta, Chris North & Kurt Luther, *An exploratory study of human performance in image geolocation tasks* (2016). HCOMP 2016 GroupSight Workshop on Human Computation for Image and Video Analysis. https://crowd.cs.vt.edu/wp-content/uploads/2016/10/cxploratory-study-human_camera_ready.pdf

36 Ole Alexander Saue, *Dagbladet journalist Angelica Hagen occasionally knocks on strangers' doors to find good stories [Av og til banker Dagbladet-journalist Angelica Hagen på fremmedes dører for å finne gode saker]* (26 April 2019). Retrieved 18 November 2019 from Medier24 medier24.no/artikler/av-og-til-banker-dagbladet-journalist-angelica-hagen-pa-fremmedes-dorer-for-a-finne-gode-saker/463029

37 Benjamin Strick (Director of Investigations at the Centre for Information Resilience, previously an investigative journalist for BBC Africa Eye and affiliated with Bellingcat), personal communication, 16 April 2020.
38 Sector035, *Chronolocation of Media* 2(26 November 2021). Retrieved 31 August 2023 from Sector035 sector035.nl/articles/chronolocation-of-media
39 Benjamin Strick's video guide: *OSINT At Home #8 – Calculate time using shadows in a photo or video* (1. March 2021). Retrieved 28. August 2023 from YouTube youtube.com/watch?v=9z26rSP2eqs
40 Ibid.
41 Craig Silverman, *Investigating Digital Mis/Disinformation GIJN19* (28 September 2019). Retrieved 12 January 2020 from Google Docs docs.google.com/presentation/d/1vrh9h3IC7hI9LwfxfQmZ5yfZL0Cu7CzurFPepQpbbVs/edit#slide=id.g6197b3c15d_2_81
42 Fergus Bell, *Verification: Source vs. Content* (14 December 2018). Retrieved 24 September 2019 from Medium medium.com/@ferg/verification-source-vs-content-b67d6eed3ad0
43 The proposal is made by Heidi Tworek in *Responsible Reporting in an Age of Irresponsible Information* (23 March 2018). Retrieved 11 September 2019 from Alliance For Securing Democracy securingdemocracy.gmfus.org/responsible-reporting-in-an-age-of-irresponsible-information
44 Claire Wardle, *A journalist's guide to working with social sources* (September 2016). Retrieved 10 September 2019 from First Draft firstdraftnews.org/wp-content/uploads/2016/09/First-Draft-A-Journalists-Guide-To-Approaching-Social-Sources.pdf, p. 6.
45 Milena Marin, *Sending encrypted photos while preserving metadata* (20 April 2020). Retrieved 1 May 2020 from Amnesty International Citizen Evidence Lab citizenevidence.org/2020/04/20/sending-encrypted-photos-while-preserving-metadata
46 Eurovision News, *Clearance for Eurovision News Exchange* (undated). Retrieved 9 December 2019 from Eurovision News Exchange news-exchange.ebu.ch/clearance
Storyful, *Storyful Content Agreement* (undated). Retrieved 9 December 2019 from Storyful storyful.com/clearance
47 Casey Newton has written about Facebook and YouTube's content moderators in a series of articles titled *The Terror Queue* (16 December 2019). Retrieved 17 December 2019 from The Verge theverge.com/2019/12/16/21021005/google-youtube-moderators-ptsd-accenture-violent-disturbing-content-interviews-video
Osman Kibar offers a peek into the daily life of Norwegian content moderators working from Malta in *A hidden billion-dollar industry: The digital laundry aids [Skjult milliardindustri: De digitale vaskehjelpene]* (9 September 2016). Retrieved 17 December 2019 from Dagens

Næringsliv dn.no/magasinet/dokumentar/facebook/peter-munster/sensur/skjult-milliardindustri-de-digitale-vaskehjelpene/1-1-5724969.

48 Casey Newton, *YouTube moderators are being forced to sign a statement acknowledging the job can give them PTSD* (24. January 2020). Retrieved 16 April 2020 from The Verge theverge.com/2020/1/24/21075830/youtube-moderators-ptsd-accenture-statement-lawsuits-mental-health

49 Casey Newton, *Facebook will pay $52 million in settlement with moderators who developed PTSD on the job* (12 May 2020). Retrieved 26 May 2020 from The Verge theverge.com/2020/5/12/21255870/facebook-content-moderator-settlement-scola-ptsd-mental-health

50 Anthony Feinstein, Blair Audet & Elizabeth Waknine, *Witnessing images of extreme violence: a psychological study of journalists in the newsroom* (2014). JRSM Open doi.org/10.1177/2054270414533323

51 Sam Dubberley, Elizabeth Griffin & Haluk Mert Bal, *Making Secondary Trauma a Primary Issue: A Study of Eyewitness Media and Vicarious Trauma on the Digital Frontline* (November 2015). Retrieved 24 October 2019 from Eyewitness Media Hub eyewitnessmediahub.com/research/vicarious-trauma

52 The advice was original published following an interview with Bell on NRKbeta in conjunction with the coverage – *I hit a massive wall [– Jeg gikk på en solid smell]* (10 April 2016). Retrieved 24 September 2019 from NRKbeta nrkbeta.no/2016/04/10/jeg-gikk-pa-en-solid-smell

53 Fergus Bell, *Get it out the door fast ... and right* (6 August 2015). Retrieved 24 October 2019 from Medium medium.com/@ferg/get-it-out-the-door-fast-and-right-1bd1b9b855ad

4 Journalism, online open-source investigations and OSINT

Introduction

The book has covered three things so far: 1) evaluation of sources, 2) why evaluation of sources is important and 3) how digital source evaluation methods can be used to assure the quality of media content from the Internet. In this chapter, we direct our critical gaze outward and into the future of the digital age. We will look at how the idea of source criticism can be applied to the work of discovering new material, and not solely the evaluation of incoming content. Navigating all the open sources on the Internet requires advanced expertise in the evaluation of digital sources. It also requires creativity and patience. The combination of expertise in the evaluation of digital sources and creativity is the key to detecting patterns as well as additional sources that can help clarify or confirm the details of a story. In short, you must have expertise in digital source criticism to be able to ascertain the quality of information you encounter on the Internet during a research phase. You will also need this expertise to determine which websites will provide credible information.

This part of the book is mainly about how it is possible to use different open registries and databases to find and compile new information. As a journalist, using building blocks of information from a range of credible internet sources will build a strong foundation for your work. A range of simple techniques will nudge you in the right direction and help you untangle the knots of a complex news story.

Imagine that you have a telephone number but an internet search fails to identify the caller. It is possible to do a specialised web search using Google or even money transfer apps to track down the caller. This can produce hits usually filtered out of directory enquiry

DOI: 10.4324/9781003449461-5

services and help to confirm the validity of information or solve a case.[1] There are also many media archives that contain information of great value for that task of verification, which will enable you to build on the work other journalists have done. Are you searching for a person who does not appear on the Internet or in any well-known databases? Maybe there is a newspaper article that contains valuable information. As an example, more than 1 million digitised newspapers have been made available in the digital library of the Norwegian National Library.[2] The articles found here can offer supplementary historical information about people and places, which can be used to cross-check other information in the process of critically evaluating sources.

Digging through open digital sources

Join in on a thought experiment. Imagine a photo of a well-known bridge, such as London's Tower Bridge. The dominant object in the image is the structure itself. Some people can be seen walking towards it, vehicles are driving over it and buildings are under construction in the background.

As a journalist, you will often find yourself in situations that require you to determine when and where an image has been taken. Usually, this information will be embedded in a file's metadata, although as we now know, this type of data will typically be scrubbed when uploaded to major social media platforms. That is why you must think creatively. If you examine the image closely enough, it is possible that you will find enough clues there to identify the location. Perhaps you are already familiar with the area. Then the angle of the photograph will immediately reveal where the photographer was standing. The shadows of pedestrians and the height of the water line can tell you the time of year and even the day the image was taken.

Back to the example of the bridge. A large office building is being constructed in the background and is currently half-finished. Google Earth has satellite imagery from before and after the structure was built. This narrows the time frame we need to address in our analysis. A quick online search reveals that the construction firm has posted a timelapse film with date and time stamps embedded in the footage, further narrowing our time frame. In the image we can see a distinctive vessel heading out to sea. Its position can be confirmed by MarineTraffic and other, similar sources. It is a sunny day, a fact that is confirmed by checking the historical data found on WolframAlpha. You dig up a newspaper story about a traffic incident in the vicinity, the date of which suggests that it could be a potential match. A cyclist filming her daily commute has uploaded a video from her helmet camera, documenting the area around Tower Bridge in the time period before, during and after our image was taken. Just before the accident, she passes the bridge and then the spot from which the image was taken. In the video you can clearly see a person taking a photo from the same spot. The person is wearing a jacket with a company logo on it. The company website provides a list of employees, where you find and identify the person in the jacket, as well as his phone number. You call the number and are able to confirm the origin of the image.

The example is fictitious, but it demonstrates the abundance of potential sources that can be used to extract information from a video or an image. It is not always easy to determine when and where an image was taken. However, if the image has not been altered or generated, we can establish one thing: it was taken somewhere on the planet. Through the use of a bit of creative ingenuity, it is often possible to determine the exact location. It is relatively easy for someone from the Netherlands to determine whether a photograph has been taken in front of the Rijksmuseum in Amsterdam or the Erasmusbrug in Rotterdam. Identifying the location in photos from other parts of the world is more complicated. As a journalist, you will often have to do this if you work with digital and visual sources. Digital tools such as Google Street View will often allow you to navigate to the exact location in the world where a photograph was taken. Sometimes this task is difficult because the image does not contain landmarks or other clearly recognisable features and is solely a landscape or a building. Photographs taken indoors can be particularly difficult. Nonetheless, in a surprising number of cases it will be possible to determine exactly when and where a photograph was taken if you search thoroughly enough. You can start by looking for unique features in the image, such as a tower, masts, signs, letters, rivers or other details. Maybe there is a bicycle, lamp post or litter bin typical of a particular region or country somewhere in the image. How about fauna and flora? Maybe you can see window shutters reflected in a television screen or a menu lying on a table in a restaurant. Many objects can offer hints about where and when the video or image was captured.[3] This information can then be cross-checked against map data, image services, and adverts published on Airbnb etc. – here there are many possibilities.

The combination and application of digital information as outlined above has recently sparked a new wave of forensic-style journalism. Often referred to as *online open-source investigations* or *visual investigations*, the processes involved are not solely employed by journalists.[4] One term commonly in use is the traditional military acronym OSINT (open-source intelligence), which signifies a process of collecting factual information from open and public-access sources and compiling it into a single story or report. This is actually what journalism has always been about, and the introduction of the Internet has dramatically increased the number of available sources. This has also altered the possibilities journalists have to collaborate and present their work and work processes. The enormous quantity of data and information now available through the Internet can be verified and compiled to produce new knowledge, demonstrate injustice or improve the basis for decision-making. Expertise and creativity are required to find information, along with a well-developed knack for evaluating digital sources in order to determine whether the information can be trusted.

On the Internet many platforms offer satellite imagery as well as map and geolocation data. Advanced data about shipping and aviation traffic is mere keystrokes away and information is often posted on social media that is open or available to everyone with a registered user account. All of this data can potentially be combined – often along with data from other sources – to reconstruct events and environments. Some examples of open sources are:

- news websites
- public data, databases and websites
- open websites
- social media
- archive services
- the deep web – all areas of the Internet that are not indexed by standard search engines
- maps and geographical (geospatial) data
- blogs
- apps
- digital financial services (such as Venmo or crypto currency)

- video services
- academic articles.

Because search engines can neither find nor display all the information available, it can be useful to access alternative sources to find more data.[5] There are many databases or data catalogues that contain information you will not find using a search engine. Anyone can set up such databases, so you must be creative and critical when engaging with them. A good tip is to ask for guidance at a library or university. It is also possible to use search engines and combine your search words with database OR directory OR catalogue OR registry to find hints on related sites. At the end of Wikipedia articles you will often find a list of "related sites" that may contain additional information of relevance to your search.

From military to civil use

It is no longer solely the military that conducts open-source intelligence. The methods have awakened the interest of many stakeholders in both the public and private sectors, in keeping with the increasing volume of information available on the Internet. Edward Snowden's disclosures are one example that clearly illustrates how public authorities all over the world consider data from social media to be extremely valuable, and this trend is not showing signs of reversal any time soon. *The Economist* described Russia's manoeuvres during the escalation leading to the invasion of Ukraine in February 2022 as "a coming-out party for open-source intelligence".[6] A rapidly growing community of journalists, experts, analysts and amateurs were able to track Russian forces near the Ukrainian border using open sources such as satellite imagery.

The military has a long history with OSINT, and many countries have recently expanded the scale of their investment. The commander of the UK's Strategic Command, Sir James Hockenhull, reached out directly to the OSINT community to seek assistance in revising the UK army's approach to open sources and in leveraging the potential of such sources to a much greater extent.[7] While arguably a global phenomenon, open-source intelligence is on the rise in many areas of the public sector, including in Norway. The Norwegian Tax Administration, the Directorate of Immigration, the Customs Authority, the Norwegian Water Resources and Energy Directorate, the Police Security Service and the National Criminal Investigation Service are just a few of the institutions that have invested in the investigation of open sources on the Internet. After the terrorist attack of 22 July 2011 in Norway, open-source intelligence was highlighted as a specific area of focus for the Norwegian police force.[8] The assessment of the terrorist incident at the Al-Noor mosque in Norway makes reference to how the police used open sources in different components of its investigation, in addition to public registries.[9] Open sources are valuable because they can provide information simply and quickly, even information that is not available in public databases.[10] One consequence of this is that the Norwegian National Criminal Investigation Service in 2018 developed its own standards for open-source searches. These are exempt from public disclosure, but the police and the public prosecutor have access.[11] A version suited for civil society has been developed by the Human Rights Investigations Lab at the University of California, Berkeley in collaboration with the UN. It is called the Berkeley Protocol on Digital Open Source Investigations and is a set of standards and guidelines for identification, collection, storage, verification and analysis of open-source data. Such a system has become necessary because the use of internet content as evidence in legal proceedings is increasingly common.

Also in journalism, open-source intelligence has been receiving added attention in recent years. The reasons for this are not surprising and coincide with the motivations of other actors: the increase in digital sources available on the Internet and the many new tools for navigating all the information. For journalists, digging through open sources is becoming indistinguishable from the job of cultivating sources, finding confidential information and other investigative techniques involving hidden or less public sources.[12] Journalists and others who are constantly developing and updating their own abilities to search, discover, verify and analyse digital information will be equipped to deliver better and more comprehensive investigative journalism in the future.

The development within online open-source investigations has also seeped into the media industry, where it is being combined with the professional ethics, traditional practices and procedures that have long since become established aspects of investigative journalism. Openness about the methods and sources employed makes it simpler for the public to analyse what a journalist does and does not know.[13] By showing your cards, all incentives are aligned towards the promotion of more reliable journalistic work, which in turn also strengthens your credibility.[14] Openness about methods and work processes helps increase the credibility of the methods for and the results of online open-source investigations. Digital platforms also offer wholly different alternatives for the presentation of findings. This has contributed to increasing the visibility of journalistic methods, including them as part of the story being told.

The BBC started working with user-generated content early in the game and has announced that the next step is to train journalists in open-source intelligence.[15] One example of the BBC's work with digital investigation is the investigations series Africa Eye, which regularly uses a broad variety of digital sources in its editorial work. This work is not solely digital, however, and is combined with source cultivation and traditional, boots-on-the-ground journalism.

There is substantial activity in this field in journalism globally and an abundance of cases can be cited. Journalism conferences all over the world are consistently including the acronym OSINT and offer sessions that describe the methods employed in advanced digital investigative journalism. Many Norwegian media outlets have done award-winning work using open-source investigative techniques. The Norwegian national newspaper *Aftenposten* revealed that several members of the Norwegian parliament had submitted false travel receipts. The newspaper uncovered this information by checking the receipts against open sources such as the Norwegian parliament's website and Facebook.[16] Using open sources such as court documents, telephone directories, photos and social media, the newspaper also tracked down Russian double agents, which may have played a part in luring the Norwegian Frode Berg into a trap in Moscow.[17]

Open-source intelligence work in journalism cannot be defined as a single method. The practice can be compared to solving a puzzle, which can only be achieved by someone who is creatively and critically able to navigate digital information on the Internet to track down and assemble the disparate pieces. The references to Sherlock Holmes fly fast and furious in descriptions of journalist-detective-investigators who will spend hours on services such as Google Maps, Yandex Panoramas or Sentinel Hub searching for leads while working on a story. These detectives are on the verge of occupying journalism in a serious fashion. A discussion about the use of terminology is therefore underway. The use of military terms such as OSINT to describe a journalist's digital investigations is not always equally popular. The well-known journalist and researcher Margot Williams has advocated for the demilitarisation of terminology used in reference to digital investigations carried out by journalists.[18]

Complex digital investigative journalism stories

Another renowned media organisation that has invested in open-source investigation is *The New York Times*. They have recruited staff from the news agency Storyful, the investigative journalism group Bellingcat and the human rights group Human Rights Investigations Lab, to name a few, to work in the sub-brand called Visual Investigations, which works almost exclusively with open-source investigation and its visual depiction. In a video series of the same name, the Visual Investigations team reports on complex issues such as murder, smuggling and police violence through what is described as a new form of investigative and expository journalism.[19] The terms "visual forensics" and "investigative video reporting" summon associations of the investigations traditionally carried out by police and military intelligence, but the work is done by the journalists on staff who explain every step they have taken along the way. The value of the new work methods is described as lying predominantly in the coverage of difficult-to-access locations, such as war zones. The methods can also be used in cases where an abundance of video content exists that can be collected and organised, which is a relatively common phenomenon in large cities.[20]

The visual forensics team of *The New York Times* combines ordinary journalism with advanced technical methods and tools such as facial recognition, the analysis of satellite imagery, 3D reconstructions of crime scenes, and the amassing of vast quantities of photo and video content. One of the team's founders, journalist Malachy Browne, explains that the objective is to put together a complex investigation containing an extremely large number of data points targeting the broadest possible audience. Precisely because the news of today is almost always captured on camera, this type of evidence can be taken apart image by image to help reconstruct key events. The team has played a key role in the newspaper's coverage of high-profile news stories, including the Russian invasion of Ukraine and the "Pentagon leaks".

An example of the lengths to which *The New York Times* is willing to go to recreate an event is how they went door-to-door to acquire video footage from surveillance cameras in Brooklyn after the killing of 15-year-old Lesandro Guzman-Feliz. In this way they obtained evidence on film that even the police had failed to uncover in their investigation.[21] In the investigation of the killing of the nurse Rouzan al-Najjar during a demonstration in Gaza, metadata played a key role. The journalists gathered all the original content they could find on the event. They spoke with photographers who were on the scene to gain access to the contents of their memory cards – including all the metadata. They were thereby able to establish exactly when the photos and videos were captured. Because they had a presence in Gaza, *The New York Times* was able to acquire more than 1,300 photos and videos from the original devices of journalists and others who documented the demonstration during which al-Najjar was killed. All the media content was subsequently put into a single timeline in the newsroom.

This story is yet another good example of the thoroughness of *The New York Times*' approach. Once they began watching the same scene unfolding over and over again at different times on the video timeline, they sensed that something was amiss. Some of the cameras had incorrect date and time settings, so they had to track down each individual photographer before they could change these settings on their cameras. The news team then had the photographers take a photo of a precise timekeeping device and calculate the discrepancy, in order to establish the exact time and date that photos or video were captured, using the metadata.[22] With the help of drones, the news desk gathered data on the scene after the fact and built a 3D model into which photos and video segments could be inserted visually. With such a rich and detailed foundation of data, they were able to create a picture of what had taken place on the ground and identify the critical moments that caused the situation to escalate.

By gathering all this data, the visual investigations team was able to freeze the time axis and analyse the situation in suspension, aided by geospatial data. They could thereby trace the hours leading up to al-Najjar's death and find six cameras that filmed her killing. Sixty people – eyewitnesses, experts, soldiers etc. – were interviewed to confirm or refute details and potential scenarios.

Sleuthing, or digging on your own

The term *sleuthing* is used by American journalists, and not without a certain degree of pride, to describe simpler projects that use online open sources in creative ways. It is not only in the context of large investigative projects at major news outlets that advanced knowledge about source criticism is employed to produce hard-hitting journalism. The American journalist Ashley Feinberg demonstrates on a regular basis what an individual journalist can achieve using these techniques. Feinberg disclosed the secret Twitter accounts of FBI Director James Comey and the prominent senator Mitt Romney, respectively, through this type of sleuthing.[23] Feinberg's analysis of an alleged video of a US president at a hotel in Moscow attracted attention due to its thoroughness in the cross-checking of details from the video against online open sources, such as the hotel's social media updates and other videos posted online.[24] Feinberg's work is an example of just how much a journalist can accomplish using these methods. The democratisation of technology and tools means that sleuthing of this nature is not solely a strategy available to large newsrooms with enormous resources. Even small-scale news desks and journalists working alone will find these methods very useful.

Because *The New York Times* and Bellingcat have had great success utilising this strategy, they are now under governmental scrutiny. Both have stated that they keep the police and the military at arm's length when they are approached with collaboration requests. Bellingcat does not allow members of the military intelligence to attend the courses they hold, and *The New York Times* does not share its findings with the police.[25]

In light of media stakeholders' success with journalistic open-source investigations in recent years, both Columbia Journalism School's Tow Centre and Global Investigative Journalism Network have published comprehensive guides on the best procedures for carrying out these types of investigations.[26]

The process of digital investigative journalism

The workflow of the advanced digital digging carried out by journalists can be summarised in six steps. The first entails coming up with ideas, finding leads or getting tips from the general public and others. The story then moves into the research phase, typically by doing internet searches using search engines, databases or other resources where it is possible to find relevant data. A solid grasp of source criticism is important here. Relevant results and collected data must be stored so they can be located again efficiently. A growing concern is how quickly valuable documentation can be erased by large social media platforms if there is a risk of it violating their guidelines.[27] Content should be saved both locally in the newsroom and on more neutral and open sites such as Internet Archive's Wayback Machine or another third-party archiving solution. Website screenshots and archiving are imperative. Software such as Hunchly and Rewind has been created to capture everything you see on the Internet so it will be possible to return to a website even if it has disappeared since the last time you visited it. Copies of a website on Internet Archive will serve as a credible and independent source and simultaneously make the source materials available for the public at large. It is important to remember that there are different methods stakeholders can use to remove content from such web-based archiving services. A typical example would be if a copyright holder accuses the archive service of copyright violation and thereby has the content removed.

The data collected must then be subjected to the verification process described in Chapter 3 of this book, in the course of which the media content, data and sources must be investigated and scrutinised. Then the data that has been verified to a satisfactory extent must be given an editorial evaluation. Is the content relevant to the story? Is publishing the content ethically defensible? Are there any changes that must be made? Is anonymity an issue? New leads or disclosures that have emerged during the process should be evaluated at this point and pursued through new searches and repetition of the above process.

Subsequently, all the information is stitched together into visualisations and other presentation methods, which can involve text, video, photos, 3D models, animation etc. When this is to be presented to the public, you should have a well thought-out strategy for including both the input of the public and feedback that can lead to new stories through ideas, leads and tips. The process can then be repeated. Groups such as Bellingcat often do transparent investigations in which they solicit tips and help from the public throughout the process. They also engage their community regularly through online and offline events. This stands in striking contrast to the refusal to reveal tips, sources and ongoing stories both before and after publication that has been typical of more traditional investigative journalism.

Finally, it must be mentioned that journalists should think about their own operational security when conducting open-source investigations online. Internet traffic or other data that can disclose your identity or simply that you are a journalist working on a story can produce challenges. An illustrative example is that of the man who discovered he was being investigated by journalists from *The New York Times* because the newspaper's IP addresses kept appearing on his website's server logs.[28] Digital technology and open sources can also be used with malicious intent by individuals gathering information for the purpose of attacking journalists.[29] Journalists are not alone here. The Norwegian National Security Authority has singled out open sources as a potential security risk for society. One of the authority's risk reports states that "The picture painted by the compilation of openly available information illustrates that it would be sufficient to have an impact on valuable infrastructure and other functions".[30]

Debunking information posted by the president of Brazil

Let us take a look at an example of how verification work and investigation using online open sources can be combined. When Norway chose to halt its foreign aid to the Amazon rainforest in protest against the increased deforestation, Brazil's president Jair Bolsonaro responded by sharing a video on Twitter that allegedly documented the brutal slaughter of whales in Norway. Most of the large Norwegian media organisations covered the video and intimated that the whale killing documented in the video did not take place in Norway but in the Faroe Islands. No Norwegian media stated this conclusively, however, and instead included qualifiers in their coverage, using phrases such as "judging by appearances", "most likely", "probably" and "appears to come from".[31]

I was tasked with tracking down the video's sources and was able to establish categorically that the video was not made in Norway – working for the only news outlet to do so. This was accomplished by investigating open sources online. The video was made up of several film sequences and stills that were combined and presented as an incident that had taken place in Norway on a given date in 2019.

The video opens with a clip of footage from what appears to be a news broadcast. Twitter simplified the task of making contact with foreign journalists, and a Brazilian journalist could easily establish that the clip was taken from Brazil's most prominent evening news programme and was about the recent foreign aid adjustments.

The video was of extremely poor quality, which suggests that it was uploaded onto the Internet many times over. Several watermarks were visible. The Norwegian media outlet *Dagbladet* was able to link one of the watermarks to what was apparently a fan account on Twitter

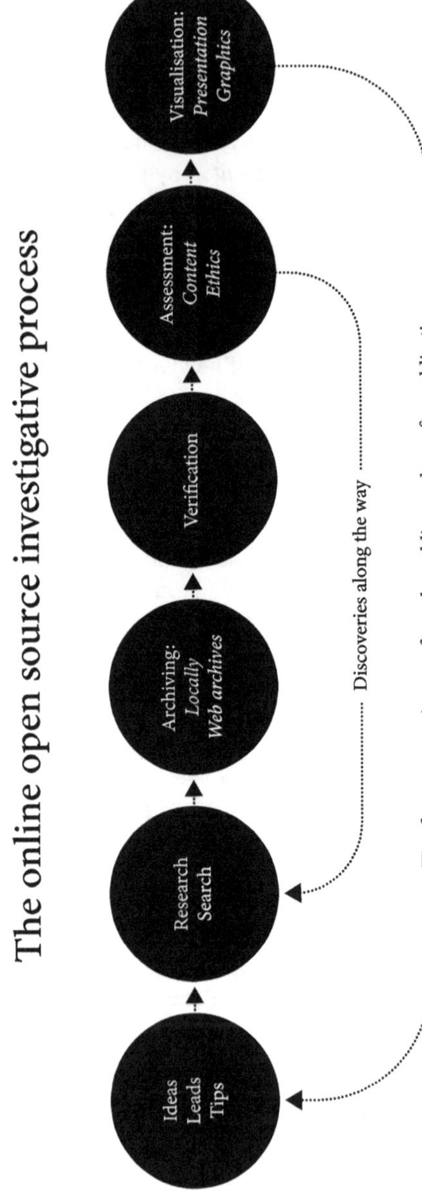

Figure 4.1 A model of the workflow for the journalistic online open-source investigative process.

that had created the video shared by the president.[32] Another watermark came from the organisation Sea Shepherd UK, which on its own social media user accounts confirmed that their videos of pilot whale hunting from Sandavágur on the Faroe Islands had been used. Based on the details from Sea Shepherd UK, identifying where on the Faroe Island the videos were made was not difficult. In Sea Shepherd's video clip, a row of houses can be seen in the background. By comparing the houses in the video with those shown on Google Street View, it was possible to confirm that the location was the same. Characteristic buildings and cranes in the harbour were also clearly visible. The video contained a series of stills, and the source of these was tracked down using a reverse image search. Finally, it was possible to refute the claim that the content was filmed in Norway on the day in question and establish the actual time and place of the video.

Creative methods for open-source investigations

There is no set formula stipulating the best method for investigating open sources. Because the volume of sources on the Internet is enormous and varied, creative problem solving is key. Let us take a look at a few different examples.

Sources on LinkedIn

When journalist Carole Cadwalladr disclosed connections between the American hedge fund manager Robert Mercer and the UK data analysis firm Cambridge Analytica, she was aware of one thing: this was not the full story. A search commenced on the social network platform LinkedIn, where Cadwalladr trawled users who had connections to the UK company.[33] LinkedIn has with time begun targeting journalists with an eye to recruiting them as power users and offered free professional accounts to journalists who took part in an online course. The platform possesses information about the places of work and university affiliations of millions of people. In Norway, Ipsos estimates that more than 1 million Norwegians have a user account on the platform.[34] This makes it a helpful resource for journalists, who can use the platform to search for former or current employees of a given enterprise. Cadwalladr eventually got a nibble on LinkedIn, and somebody suggested she contact Christopher Wylie, who had worked with Facebook data at Cambridge Analytica. The result was a year-long investigative project and an agenda-setting front page story about how Cambridge Analytica without consent had acquired access to 50 million Facebook accounts.[35]

Sources on GitHub

During the first COVID-19 lockdown in Norway, NRK journalist Øyvind Bye Skille received a tip that the company Simula on behalf of the Norwegian Institute of Public Health was developing an app to perform advanced tracking of Norwegian residents who had contracted the COVID-19 virus. It was not long before it occurred to Skille that the code for the app might be found somewhere on the Internet.[36] The platform GitHub is an indispensable tool for many programmers and a place where code can be published openly or privately. This makes cooperation with both in-house and external partners possible. Search terms related to relevant stakeholders and the app disclosed code that processed collected data on a central server. Furthermore, it was possible to download the code and investigate who had participated in its programming. By investigating these contributors, the journalist was able to determine the department in the company that had worked on the project. This type of information can be extremely valuable for journalists. When NRK published a story about its findings, the code was immediately removed from the Internet.[37]

Triangulating photos from aerial images, classified ad sites and Instagram

In conjunction with an investigative project, I was searching for information about a specific property in Norway. One website contained aerial photographs and detailed maps that showed the appearance of the buildings but no further information about the property. It was a relatively new building, and the information available on the most commonly used services was scant. The land registry revealed that the property was owned by a public Norwegian institution, but searches on Google, business websites and other directories provided no further information of significance.

The search then moved on to Norway's leading online marketplace Finn.no, to look for other properties that had been sold in the same district. A house east of the property had recently been sold. The advert on Finn was compared with photos taken from the veranda and of surroundings that could include the neighbouring house.

Several online real estate services provided information about names connected to addresses, and the social media profiles of the residents listed were explored.

I then returned to the map to look for other candidates with sightlines to the property in question. Directly north there appeared to be a good candidate, but the aerial photos revealed that there was a lot of vegetation on the grounds. By searching for clues online about the registered resident, it was possible to find relevant information. The person had a Facebook profile that was rarely updated, but the hits produced by a Google search using the person's name in quotation marks included an obscure site that indexed photos from Instagram. The site redirected to an Instagram profile in the resident's name. One of the few photos found on the profile hit the nail on the head, offering the view from the kitchen window on a winter day, where there was no foliage on trees or bushes. In addition to the snow on the property, the image provided a unique perspective of the neighbouring property. The photo showed the house from another angle, which in turn led to more information about the property.

Online marketplaces have also proven useful for Bellingcat. The group was trying to track down an audio recording of a military officer's voice. A search for the officer's face using the search engine Yandex produced a substantial number of hits and links to other photos of this person on the Internet. One of the photos came from an advert for a used television set. The photo of the television in the advert was taken at the exact moment when an interview with the officer was being broadcast. Based on the image, it was clear which television channel had done the interview. By checking the television channel's programming for the dates around the time the photo was uploaded, they got results: on the same day that the advert was posted, a documentary about the military was aired on television. When they acquired the documentary, they found that it contained a long sequence during which the officer spoke without interruption. They used this to carry out further analyses.[38]

From video to panorama

A brilliant technique for gaining an overview of the surrounding environment in a video is to convert it into a panorama photo. By exporting the individual frames from the video, you can combine these to create a large photo. Because a video is made up of 24 or more images per second, you can acquire a great deal of information from a video using this technique. A panorama photo provides a completely different overview than that of video footage panning a situation or landscape. Bellingcat associated Henk van Ess used a 35-second video of a criminal who was wanted by the police that was posted on Instagram. The video was converted into 1,200 images which were then stitched into a panorama photo. In this case,[39] the Agisoft program Metashape was used, but Adobe Photoshop and free software such as Microsoft's Image Composite Editor can also be used for this task. Although all the different elements that contributed to determining where and when the video was made (an orange dustbin, a distinctive patio, the star magnolia to the left in the photo) are visible in the video, this type of panorama image is valuable. The view of both the garden and the house was instantly enhanced, making it easier to search for the property in satellite imagery or other photos from the region.

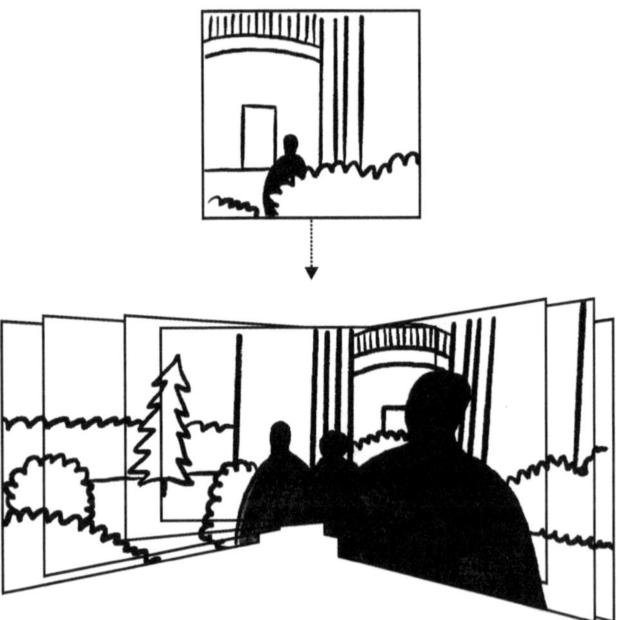

Figure 4.2 A panorama photo made of 1,200 frames from one Instagram video. Inspired by Henk van Ess.

From blurry to sharp in 500 frames

After the journalist Pavel Sheremet was killed by a car bomb in Kyiv, colleagues began gathering surveillance video footage from the area. Although they were denied access to a number of key cameras in the vicinity, they were able to find a camera with footage of the vehicle in question.[40] Because it was dark and the quality of the video was poor, only a few letters on the licence plate were legible. As a last resort, they decided to contact Bellingcat, and the 3D artist Timmi Allen was assigned to the task. Allen determined that image noise (which gives digital photos a grainy quality) from the camera sensor was the cause. After breaking the video down into individual frames, 500 of these were layered, one on top of the other. For almost two weeks, Allen experimented with adjusting the exposure and contrast of the different images and ended up with a photo in which the entire licence plate was legible.[41] Topaz and other companies also offer software such as Sharpen AI, which claim to perform a similar process automatically using machine learning. The process described by Allen is a good example of the patience often mentioned in connection with verification work and online open-source investigations.

3D models in brief

Geolocation data lies at the heart of journalistic and online open-source investigations – not merely in terms of its verification, but also in the reconstruction of events using what is known as *spatial* information. In this context, digital 3D technology stands out as a field in which journalists will be obliged to have greater expertise in the future. A number of Norwegian media outlets have used 3D models in a variety of projects. NRK's TV-broadcasts from the powerful tidal current Saltstraumen and the multi-media documentary *Fuglefjellet* about the seabird breeding season used data from the Norwegian Mapping Authority to create detailed 3D models of the landscape as supporting documentation for journalism. NRK's Harald Jansson used Blender, a free and open-source software program for 3D modelling, to create the model. In Blender you can retrieve data from large mapping databases or specialised maps to build models of an area containing altitude profiles and other elements.[42]

The newspaper VG's multi-media feature about the frigate Helge Ingstad collision combined 3D models of the vessels involved and of the surrounding region, nautical maps, open position data and radar data, and an audio log the newspaper had acquired through closed sources. When combined, these open and closed sources created a composite overview of the situation at the moment when the apparently inexplicable collision occurred in Hjeltefjorden, Norway. VG's programmer Einar Otto Stangvik created the model using Unity, software originally designed for game development but increasingly employed for other purposes.[43]

It is also possible to create your own 3D models. 3D scanning has predominantly been the preserve of experts with access to expensive equipment but has with time become available on handheld scanners, ordinary camera equipment, cell phones and drones.[44] Traditionally, photogrammetry is used to create models of actual objects, such as aerial photos, cartography and architecture. Use of the method has gradually become prevalent in police investigations and in the development of games like *Call of Duty*.[45] The latest cell phones equipped with several cameras and sensors have capacity for relatively advanced 3D scanning. This has opened up new opportunities for journalism.

In recent years, *The New York Times* has experimented with 3D scanning and modelling to tell stories based on multi-dimensional models.[46] The newspaper reports that 3D technology, along with virtual reality (VR) and augmented reality (AR), offer "a new level of remote access and an understanding of crime scenes that can substantially improve investigations of human rights violations". You can thereby expand your repertoire from tired satellite imagery to include a variety of visual data sources. These can be presented as animated objects in web videos, 3D elements in online stories, or AR experiences for cell phones and tablets.

Three cases of investigative reporting in which open sources played a major role

As the media have begun implementing open sources in new ways, many impressive stories have also been produced. To illustrate some examples of the breadth of themes and methods, we will now look at three cases in detail. At the time of publication, all the stories included lengthy video documentaries explaining the story with abundant illustrations of the methods used and sources. It is recommended that the reader study these videos for a thorough introduction to how digital investigative reporting was used in each individual case.

"Anatomy of a Killing" by BBC Africa Eye

The BBC Africa Eye video "Anatomy of a Killing" is a textbook example of how traditional journalism and online open-source investigations can go hand in hand. The starting point was a viral video of the abduction and murder of two women and two children by a group of soldiers. In the wake of speculations about whether the video was from Mali or Cameroon, the Cameroonian authorities denied the involvement of their soldiers and called it fake news. The BBC investigated the story, as did Bellingcat, Amnesty and independent analysts.[47]

A distinctive mountain formation is visible at the start of the video. Because services such as Google Earth combine satellite imagery and altitude data, the journalists had no trouble searching for the mountain formation on the Internet. However, it was a tip from a source that put them on the trail of a possible location for the mountain range, which led to a match on the outskirts of a village on the border between Cameroon and Nigeria. There are a number of features in this area that correspond with satellite imagery and the video: the mountain formation, the trail they are walking on, buildings and vegetation. Once the location was established, the time of the video had to be determined. A building was visible in the video, but satellite imagery showed that the building was half-finished in 2014 and razed in 2016. In other words, the video was made at a moment sometime between these two dates. Due to the climate, the dry trail they are walking on is only visible in satellite imagery between January and April every year, which indicates that the video is from early 2015. By calculating the angle of the soldiers' shadows on the ground, the date could be narrowed down to sometime between 20 March and 5 April 2015.

The journalists subsequently addressed the identities of the soldiers. By investigating the types of weapons, uniforms and (the lack of) equipment, it was determined that they were probably from a military outpost in the vicinity. When the authorities announced the arrest of seven individuals and revealed their identities, the BBC procured more information from social media. Using this and the video, they were able to identify the culprits.

Using online open sources in its journalism, the BBC was able to prove the exact location of the killings by identifying the surrounding landscape; the time of the killings by reading the angle of the soldiers' shadows on the ground; the identity of the perpetrators through social media profiles; and finally, they were able to confirm that the executions were connected to counterterrorism operations targeting the terrorist group Boko Haram.[48] Several soldiers were later arrested.[49] The BBC's video was instrumental in the US decision to revoke USD 17 million in funding to the Cameroonian army and an EU Parliament Resolution condemning "torture, forced disappearances and extrajudicial killings perpetrated by governmental forces".[50]

"Mapping the Las Vegas Massacre" by **The New York Times'** *Visual Investigations*

In this case, *The New York Times*' Visual Investigations team covered the deadliest mass shooting committed by a single person in the USA. In the digital investigations we have considered in this section, the timeline often constitutes the backbone of the story, and this case is no exception. The attack took place in the evening, from a hotel window far above the ground facing an open square where a festival was taking place. No clear motive had been established. All of these factors contributed to making the situation chaotic for a long time after the shooting. Reports from such incidents are by and large based on official statements from the police and authorities. Because the explanations kept changing, the newsroom wanted to create its own overview, independent of the timeline presented by the Las Vegas police.[51] The newspaper therefore used a series of videos made by the public, eyewitnesses and the police to create its own timeline of the event. The media content was taken from social media and other sources and subsequently verified. All content from news agencies had already been verified by these agencies. This resulted in more than one hour of video footage and two hours of recordings from police and fire department radio communication which could be situated on the timeline chronologically.

The 12 volleys fired during the attack made up the scaffolding for the timeline. By analysing the video clips, 30 clips could be put together with absolute precision based on visible timekeeping devices in the videos (the time shown on a car dashboard, mobile phones, information screens etc.) or the video file and the sound of the gunshots.[52] In this way it was possible to reconstruct the 10-minute duration of the attack with the help of user-generated content.

The key to how *The New York Times* succeeded in telling this story is found in the combination of traditional journalism work with digital source criticism and digital visual narrative tools. Google Earth Studio provided the basis for the 3D model that was used in the final 11-minute video documentary. Journalists who had formerly served in the military helped to verify the gunshots in the audio clips, and the newspaper's journalists on the ground in Las Vegas were able to confirm details at the scene. This enabled the newsroom to establish, down to the second, when the first shot was fired. For this, the story won an Emmy in the category "Outstanding New Approaches: Current News".

"The Grenfell Tower Fire" by Forensic Architecture

More than 70 people died and over 100 were injured when a fire broke out in the 24-storey apartment building Grenfell Tower in London. The fire was visible from many parts of the city, which resulted in an enormous amount of video footage from both professional and amateur sources. Just as the overabundance of information on the Internet will not necessarily provide an accurate understanding of a sequence of events, in this case the video footage had to be combined in an expedient manner to tell the story of what actually transpired. Forensic Architecture at Goldsmiths, University of London is no traditional newsroom, but their expansive web-based experience is inspirational, on the force of its example of what can be achieved by gathering and compiling data from open sources and the general public.

Instead of piecing together events, Forensic Architecture reconstructs the scenes of human rights violations, explosions and injustice. Bombed or demolished buildings and environments are not merely viewed as illustrations of something that allegedly took place. Instead, the group proceeds on the basis of the premise that "forensic architecture" can transform ruins into a source of information about historic events.[53] The group implements spatial data in combination with open sources and digital data from cameras, sensors etc. The collected evidence is combined and situated in time and space to create a single story, in the form of physical exhibitions, internet videos or more complex web experiences, such as in this case.

According to Forensic Architecture, every video made of the apartment building while it was in flames constitutes a clue to the evolution of the fire. The group has therefore gathered a large number of videos and mapped out where and when they were captured. They also issued a call for footage from the general public. On the website that collects such videos, they asked the individuals submitting materials for descriptions or contextual information. Is it the original file? Is the time of day indicated on the footage correct? Where was the video filmed? They also gathered further information from the authorities through formal requests for access. The videos were subsequently stabilised using the program Cinema 4D and mapped onto a virtual 3D model of the building created using the free software Blender. In order to understand the process of the fire, the most essential information is what happened early on, which was documented by unstable, handheld cameras until professionals and more stable cameras subsequently arrived at the scene.[54] As a result, Forensic Architecture is now in possession of a continuous 3D video of the fire. When this is released, the public will purportedly be able navigate the videos of the fire through an interactive timeline and simultaneously view data from the emergency services, testimonies from witnesses and updates from social media in real time.

Dramatically effective methods

These are some of the ways newsrooms and other organisations have applied digital source criticism to open online sources to gather information for the coverage of different stories. Many of these techniques, combined with journalism, represent groundbreaking work in the world of news and have therefore both won prizes and led to an increased investment in such investigative techniques. The most important difference between the many organisations and newsrooms that work in this way is press ethics. A journalist is obliged to take into account a number of ethical considerations before releasing information to the public, revealing people's identities or suggesting causality. All details must be checked thoroughly.

An example from Bellingcat illustrates this point well. When a car bomb exploded in Baghdad on 30 October 2016, news agencies such as AP and Reuters reported that eight people were killed and more than 30 wounded.[55] But shortly thereafter a video from a nearby surveillance camera was posted on the Internet. In the video a car explodes, and a number of people subsequently run into the frame, lie down on the ground and pretend to be wounded. Bellingcat was quick to label the story as suspicious and enlisted help from the public in gathering information to support their claim.[56] Although they did not get to the bottom of the events surrounding the video, they succeeded in drawing attention to it.

It wasn't until several years later that the explanation for the strange incident was made public: it was an undercover operation staged by Iraqi intelligence in an attempt to trick IS into believing that its own attack had been successful.[57] Publishing these types of speculations and information would obviously have put a covert mission such as this at risk. Because an online open-source investigation can potentially be so effective that it throws a wrench in the machinery of ongoing criminal investigations, operating outside the bounds of the guidelines for press ethics represents a particular challenge.

In conclusion, I will provide a cautionary example. It is not unusual for amateurs to join forces and coordinate their efforts on social media to hunt down suspects in the context of criminal investigations. We saw an example of the negative repercussions of this form of vigilantism during the hunt for the perpetrators following the Boston Marathon bombing in 2013. With the help of more or less improvised online open-source investigations, coupled with faulty coordination and quality assurance, unconfirmed and inaccurate information regarding potential suspects quickly surfaced on the Internet. Inaccurate information spread rapidly on both social and traditional media, and the FBI consequently issued a statement to the media requesting that restraint be exercised in the reporting of unconfirmed information.[58] On social media the hunt escalated out of control, and the wrong person was incriminated on Reddit, which naturally led to a great deal of difficulty for this person's family.[59] Reddit later apologised for the platform's role in the dissemination of misinformation, and the moderators expressed remorse, such as in the documentary *The Thread* from 2015.[60]

Questions for reflection and exercises

- Can you find a news story in local or international media that uses information from online open sources? What sources were used and how were they presented in the story?
- Set up some information categories, such as geolocation data, weather data and traffic data. Can you list five different reliable sources of information in each category that can help confirm or disprove information you possess?
- Watch the mini documentary "Anatomy of a Killing" produced by BBC Africa Eye. Which of the methods employed there are new

to you? Can you imagine how you could use the same methods in your own work?

- Create your own list of experts for future use. Do you know any image editing, cartography or 3D graphics experts you could contact if you were to hit a wall when reporting on a story? Are there any local historians where you live whom you could query about details that appear in a photo or video footage? Remember that amateurs sometimes have valuable knowledge and may be able to provide you with assistance on a project.
- Become acquainted with the international professional OSINT community. Are there any individuals there who inspire you? Make a habit of following these individuals' websites or social media accounts to keep abreast of the most recent examples and methods used. The latter might suddenly prove relevant to your own work.

Notes

1 Trude Furuly & Henrik Lied, *Method report Data-SKUP 2018: Hunting "the spider" [Metoderapport Data-SKUP 2018: Jakten på "Edderkoppen"]* (2018). Retrieved 16 April 2020 from SKUP skup.no/sites/default/files/metoderapport/2018-10/Edderkoppen%2C%20NRK.pdf

2 Nasjonalbiblioteket, *New deal enables open access to 500,000 newspapers online [Ny avtale gir åpen tilgang til 500 000 aviser på nett]* (14 February 2020). Retrieved 13 April 2020 from National Library of Norway nb.no/artikler/ny-avtale-gir-apen-tilgang-til-500-000-aviser-pa-nett

3 Gerard Janssen, *Every country with a bad conscience should fear Christiaan Triebert [Elk land met een slecht geweten moet vrezen voor Christiaan Triebert]* (20 December 2018). Retrieved 4 August 2019 from Vrij Nederland vn.nl/christiaan-triebert

4 Nina C. Müller & Jenny Wiik, *From Gatekeeper to Gate-opener: Open-Source Spaces in Investigative Journalism* (2023). Journalism Practice, 17:2, 189–208, doi.org/10.1080/17512786.2021.1919543
Kelly Gates, *Day of Rage: Forensic journalism and the US Capitol riot* (2023). Media, Culture & Society, 0(0). doi.org/10.1177/01634437231188449

5 Egil Fossum & Sidsel Meyer, *Er nå det så sikkert? [How can you be so sure?]* (2008). Cappelen Damm Akademisk.
Leonie Kijewski, *How to Become a Deep Web Super Sleuth* (26 September 2019). Retrieved 28 September 2019 from Global Investigative Journalism Conference 2019 gijc2019.org/2019/09/26/become-a-deep-web-super-sleuth

6 The Economist, *A new era of transparent warfare beckons* (18 February 2022). Retrieved 8 August 2023 from The Economist economist.com/briefing/2022/02/18/a-new-era-of-transparent-warfare-beckons
7 General Sir Jim Hockenhull, *How open-source intelligence has shaped the Russia-Ukraine war* (9 December 2022). Retrieved 8 August 2023 from GOV.UK gov.uk/government/speeches/how-open-source-intelligence-has-shaped-the-russia-ukraine-war
8 Knut Storberget, *Innstilling fra Den særskilte komité om redegjørelse fra justisministeren og forsvarsministeren i Stortingets møte 10. November 2011 om angrepene 22. juli* [*Recommendation from The Special Committee regarding report from the Minister of Justice and Minister of Defence at the 10 November 2011 sitting of the Norwegian Storting on the July 22 attacks.]* (1 March 2012). Retrieved 27 September 2019 from Stortinget stortinget.no/no/Saker-og-publikasjoner/Publikasjoner/Innstillinger/Stortinget/2011-2012/inns-201112-207
9 Anja Dalgaard-Nielsen et al., *Evaluation of the police's and PST's response to the terrorist incident in Bærum on 10 August 2019 [Evaluering av politiets og PSTs håndtering av terrorhendelsen i Bærum 10. august 2019]* (29 June 2020). Retrieved 31 July 2020 from Politiet politiet.no/globalassets/04-aktuelt-tall-og-fakta/al-noor---terrorhandlingen/evaluering_terrorhendelsen_i_baerum_01072020_original_digital.pdf
10 Bjørn Rasmussen, *A source of concern or enlightenment?: Police perceptions of open internet sources for investigative purposes [Kilde til bekymring eller opplysning?: Politiets oppfatninger av åpne internettkilder til etterforskningsformål]* (2019). Retrieved from the Norwegian Police University College phs.brage.unit.no/phs-xmlui/handle/11250/2622415
11 Morten Stenstadvold et al., *The use of search in open sources at UDI and UNE [Bruk av søk i åpne kilder i UDI og UNE]* (29 April 2019). Retrieved 27 September 2019 from the Norwegian Directorate of Immigration udi.no/globalassets/global/forskning-fou_i/beskyttelse/bruk-av-sok-i-apne-kilder-i-udi-og-une.pdf
12 Craig Silverman & Rina Tsubaki, *Verification Handbook for Investigative Reporting* (15 April 2015). Retrieved 1 November 2019 from European Journalism Centre verificationhandbook.com/book2
13 Egil Fossum & Sidsel Meyer, *Er nå det så sikkert? [How can you be so sure?]* (2008). Cappelen Damm Akademisk, p. 97.
14 Ibid.
15 Tony Hall, *BBC – Tony Hall's speech at News Xchange 2018–Media Centre* (14 November 2018). Retrieved 25 September 2019 from BBC Media Centre bbc.co.uk/mediacentre/speeches/tony-hall-news-xchange-2018
16 Henning Carr Ekroll et al., *Aftenposten reveals: Top Progress party official submitted fictitious travel bills to parliament [Aftenposten avslører: Frp-profil leverte fiktive reiseregninger til Stortinget]* (17 October 2018).

Retrieved 12 January 2020 from Aftenposten aftenposten.no/norge/politikk/i/Rx0GR2/aftenposten-avsloerer-frp-profil-leverte-fiktive-reiseregninger-til-stortinget

17 Per Anders Johansen et al., *The hunt for the double agents who tricked Norwegian intelligence leads to Natalja and Vasilij on the Red Square [Jakten på dobbeltagentene som lurte norsk etterretning, fører til Natalja og Vasilij på Den røde plass]* (5 November 2019). Retrieved 12 January 2020 from Aftenposten aftenposten.no/verden/i/4qG2aa/jakten-paa-dobbeltagentene-som-lurte-norsk-etterretning-foerer-til-natalja-og-vasilij-paa-den-roede-plass

18 Margot Williams, *This is whst[sic] THEY call OSINT. Choose your words. Demilitarize our research.* (31 July 2020). Retrieved 5 September 2020 from Twitter twitter.com/MargotWilliams/status/1288991979657977856

19 The New York Times, *Visual Investigations™ at The New York Times* (11 September 2018). Retrieved 27 September 2019 from The New York Times nytimes.com/interactive/2018/world/visual-investigations.html

20 Malachy Browne, *Reporting on Las Vegas, Pixel by Pixel* (23 October 2017). Retrieved 2 October 2019 from The New York Times nytimes.com/2017/10/23/insider/reporting-on-las-vegas-pixel-by-pixel.html

21 Malachy Browne & Anjali Singhvi, *GIJC19 – Visual Forensics: 3D Reconstruction & In-Depth Investigation* (10 October 2019). Retrieved 5 November 2019 from YouTube youtube.com/watch?v=UxX54QHTvSc

22 Ibid.

23 Andrew Beaujon, *How Ashley Feinberg Found Mitt Romney's Secret Twitter Account* (22 October 2019). Retrieved 25 October 2019 from Washingtonian washingtonian.com/2019/10/22/how-ashley-feinberg-found-mitt-romneys-secret-twitter-account

24 Ashley Feinberg, *The Pee Tape Is Real, but It's Fake* (26 September 2019). Retrieved 5 October 2019 from Slate Magazine slate.com/news-and-politics/2019/09/inside-the-convincing-fake-trump-pee-tape.html

25 Ned Beauman, *How to Conduct an Open-Source Investigation, According to the Founder of Bellingcat* (30 August 2018). Retrieved 1 October 2019 from The New Yorker newyorker.com/culture/culture-desk/how-to-conduct-an-open-source-investigation-according-to-the-founder-of-bellingcat

Malachy Browne & Anjali Singhvi, *GIJC19 – Visual Forensics: 3D Reconstruction & In-Depth Investigation* (10 October 2019). Retrieved 5 November 2019 from YouTube youtube.com/watch?v=UxX54QHTvSc

26 GIJN, *Citizen Investigation Guide* (20 September 2019). Retrieved 5 October 2019 from Global Investigative Journalism Network gijn.org/citizen-investigation-guide

Michael Edison Hayden, *A Guide to Open Source Intelligence* (OSINT) (7 June 2019). Retrieved 13 April 2020 from Columbia Journalism Review cjr.org/tow_center_reports/guide-to-osint-and-hostile-communities.php

27 This is well on its way to becoming a widely established concern in the field and is regularly addressed.
Megha Rajagopalan, *The Histories Of Today's Wars Are Being Written On Facebook And YouTube. But What Happens When They Get Taken Down?* (22 December 2018). Retrieved 7 October 2019 from BuzzFeed News buzzfeednews.com/article/meghara/facebook-youtube-icc-war-crimes
Jack Goodman and Maria Korenyuk, *AI: War crimes evidence erased by social media platforms* (1 June 2023). Retrieved 8 August 2023 from BBC News bbc.com/news/technology-65755517

28 Patrick Howell O'Neill, *How a New York Times journalist exposed an IP address and tipped off a major investigation* (16 February 2017). Retrieved 13 April 2020 from CyberScoop cyberscoop.com/new-york-times-journalist-exposed-ip-address-tipped-off-major-investigation

29 Joseph Guay with Lisa Rudnick in Sam Dubberley, Alexa Koenig & Daragh Murray, *Digital Witness* (2020). Oxford University Press, p. 294.

30 Norwegian National Security Authority (NSM), *Risk 2020 [Risiko 2020]* (17 April 2020). Retrieved 17 April 2020 from NSM nsm.stat.no/globalassets/rapporter/rapport-om-sikkerhetstilstanden/nsm-risiko-2020.pdf

31 Ståle Grut, *Sourcing Brazilian President Jair Bolsonaro's fake video seeking to hurt Norway after Amazon Fallout* (24 August 2019). Retrieved 3 April 2020 from Medium medium.com/@stalebg/sourcing-brazilian-president-jair-bolsonaros-fake-video-seeking-to-hurt-norway-after-amazon-c01e6f80ac98

32 Jesper Nordahl Finsveen, *Jair Bolsonaro: Targets Norway with bloody video [Jair Bolsonaro: Hetser Norge med blodig video]* (19 August 2019). Retrieved 12 April 2020 from Dagbladet dagbladet.no/nyheter/hetser-norge-med-blodig-video/71503270

33 Charlotte Tobitt, *Observer's Carole Cadwalladr: I became a "news slave" in pursuing Cambridge Analytica data harvesting scoop* (22 March 2018). Retrieved 3 April 2020 from Press Gazette pressgazette.co.uk/observers-carole-cadwalladr-i-became-a-news-slave-in-pursuing-cambridge-analytica-data-harvesting-scoop

34 Ipsos, *Ipsos SoMe-tracker Q2'23* (8 August 2023). Retrieved 23 October 2023 from Ipsos ipsos.com/sites/default/files/ct/publication/documents/2023-08/Ipsos%20SoMe-tracker%20Q2%202023.pdf

35 Carole Cadwalladr & Emma Graham-Harrison, *Revealed: 50 million Facebook profiles harvested for Cambridge Analytica in major data breach* (17 March 2018). Retrieved 3 April 2020 from The Guardian theguardian.com/news/2018/mar/17/cambridge-analytica-facebook-influence-us-election

36 Øyvind Bye Skille, personal communication, 24 March 2020.

37 Øyvind Bye Skille, *FHI's app will store information about your movements for 30 days [FHI-app skal lagre info om dine bevegelser i 30*

dager] (27 March 2020). Retrieved 3 April 2020 from NRK nrk.no/norge/fhi-app-skal-lagre-info-om-dine-bevegelser-i-30-dager-1.14963187

38 Bellingcat Investigation Team, *Key MH17 Figure Identified As Senior FSB Official: Colonel General Andrey Burlaka* (28 April 2020). Retrieved 1 May 2020 from Bellingcat bellingcat.com/news/2020/04/28/burlaka

39 Henk van Ess, *Locating The Netherlands' Most Wanted Criminal By Scrutinising Instagram* (19 March 2019). Retrieved 6 November 2019 from Bellingcat bellingcat.com/news/uk-and-europe/2019/03/19/locating-the-netherlands-most-wanted-criminal-by-scrutinising-instagram

40 Yana Kazmirenko, *Solving a Journalist's Murder – The Making of "Killing Pavel»* (8 May 2018). Retrieved 6 November 2019 from Global Investigative Journalism Network gijn.org/2018/05/08/making-killing-pavel-documentary-production-tips

41 The segment in which Allen explains the technique begins at the 26:55-minute mark in the video from the Organized Crime and Corruption Reporting Project, *Killing Pavel* (10 May 2017). Retrieved 6 November 2019 from YouTube youtube.com/watch?v=liSa5OFCkf4. The technique was also used when Allen analysed surveillance video footage of Saudi Arabia's consulate in conjunction with the murder of journalist Jamal Khashoggi.

42 The software add-on BlenderGIS is created specifically for importing this type of geodata into Blender.

43 Ole Petter Baugerød Stokke, *This is how VG made the ski game Løype [Slik lagde VG skispillet Løype]* (11 March 2019). Retrieved 1 October 2019 from Kode24 kode24.no/a/70842946

44 Marius Arnesen, *How to create 3D models with a drone [Slik lager du 3D-modeller med en drone]* (27 May 2015). Retrieved 10 December 2019 from NRKbeta nrkbeta.no/2015/05/27/slik-lager-du-3d-modeller-med-en-drone

45 Jesper Nordahl Finsveen, *This is why the police 3D scanned the billionaire couple's plot [Derfor 3D-skannet politiet milliardærparets tomt]* (1 February 2019). Retrieved 25 October 2019 from Dagbladet dagbladet.no/a/70721929

Mike Hume, *'Going dark' in a 'big ball of light.' A look into the making of Call of Duty: Modern Warfare* (17 October 2019). Retrieved 26 October 2019 from Washington Post Launcher washingtonpost.com/graphics/2019/video-games/call-of-duty-modern-warfare-behind-the-scenes

46 Malachy Browne et al., *How We Created a Virtual Crime Scene to Investigate Syria's Chemical Attack* (24 June 2018). Retrieved 30 September 2019 from The New York Times nytimes.com/interactive/2018/06/24/world/middleeast/douma-syria-chemical-attack-augmented-reality-ar-ul.html

47 Peabody Awards, *Anatomy of a Killing (BBC)* (2019). Retrieved 10 December 2019 from Peabody Awards peabodyawards.com/award-profile/anatomy-of-a-killing

48 BBC, *Cameroon atrocity: Finding the soldiers who killed this woman* (24 September 2018). Retrieved 10 December 2019 from BBC News bbc.com/news/av/world-africa-45599973/cameroon-atrocity-finding-the-soldiers-who-killed-this-woman

49 Josiane Kouagheu, *Cameroon probes video showing security forces apparently executing civilians* (10 August 2018). Retrieved 24 October 2019 from Reuters reuters.com/article/us-cameroon-security-video-idUSKBN1KV224

50 Amelia Fernandez-Grandon, *BBC Africa Eye celebrates one year of award-winning investigations* (30 May 2019). Retrieved 11 December 2019 from BBC Media Centre bbc.co.uk/mediacentre/latestnews/2019/africa-eye-one-year

51 Malachy Browne, *Reporting on Las Vegas, Pixel by Pixel* (23 October 2017). Retrieved 2 October 2019 from The New York Times nytimes.com/2017/10/23/insider/reporting-on-las-vegas-pixel-by-pixel.html

52 Malachy Browne, "*7/ Verify burst patterns by lining up the burst audio waveforms. Note the bullet spikes, patterns and pauses in these different videos*" (23 October 2017). Retrieved 2 October 2019 from Twitter twitter.com/malachybrowne/status/922573628566331392

53 Eyal Weizman et al., *Forensic Architecture* (2010). Architectural Design, 80(5), 58–63. doi.org/10.1002/ad.1134

54 Phoebe Braithwaite, *Can digital forensics help us work out what happened at Grenfell?* (22 March 2018). Retrieved 3 October 2019 from Wired UK wired.co.uk/article/grenfell-media-archive-forensic-architecture-sky-news

55 Maher Chmaytelli, *Car bomb kills at least eight in Baghdad market - police, medics* (30 October 2016). Retrieved 24 October 2019 from *Reuters* uk.reuters.com/article/uk-mideast-crisis-iraq-blast-idUKKBN12U0KE

56 Christiaan Triebert, *The Remarkable Case of an Iraqi Car Bomb* (4 November 2016). Retrieved 26 October 2020 from Bellingcat bellingcat.com/news/mena/2016/11/04/remarkable-case-iraqi-car-bomb

57 The New Zealand Herald, *Fake bombs and actors playing dead: The world's most dangerous undercover operation* (26 August 2018). Retrieved 28 October 2019 from NZ Herald nzherald.co.nz/world/news/article.cfm?c_id=2&objectid=12114272

58 Marisa Guthrie, *Boston Marathon Bombing: Rush to Break News Burns CNN, Fox New* (17 April 2013). Retrieved 17 April 2020 from Hollywood Reporter hollywoodreporter.com/news/cnn-boston-marathon-bombing-mistake-441551

59 Dave Lee, *Internet detectives get it wrong* (19 April 2013). Retrieved 17 April 2020 from BBC News bbc.com/news/technology-22214511
60 Laura Miller, *The Boston Marathon and Reddit: When the Internet's deluded amateur-hour detectives ran amok* (16 April 2015). Retrieved 11 January 2021 from Salon salon.com/2015/04/15/the_boston_marathon_and_reddit_when_the_internets_deluded_amateur_hour_detectives_ran_amok

Glossary

Algorithm – In the fields of mathematics and data processing, an algorithm is a precise formula specifying how a task is to be carried out.[1]

Bot – Abbreviation for software robot, which in this book usually refers to automated user accounts on social media that perform tasks such as spreading content. An algorithm commonly lies behind such bots which automatically produce content or interact with other users.[2]

Chronolocation – A method used to establish the date and time when a video was made or photo taken, without any information beyond the contents of the video or photo.

Deepfake – Constructed (and often incorrect) media content created using machine learning (artificial intelligence).

Disinformation – Information that is false and created for the purpose of disseminating particular views, provoking a specific response from recipients or causing harm to individuals, groups, organisations or countries.[3]

Erroneous information – Information based on credible content but presented or contextualised in such a way so as to undermine that content's credibility. This can be done to harm an individual, groups, organisations or countries.[4]

Fake user account – A user account on social media that assumes a false identity.

Manipulated content – Authentic content or images that are tampered with or altered for the purpose of deceiving readers or viewers.[5]

Misinformation – Incorrect information that has not been created or spread for the express purpose of misleading or causing harm. This can be a matter of misunderstandings or unconfirmed speculations.[6]

Open-source intelligence (OSINT) – The gathering of information from open sources, traditionally carried out by the military or the public authorities.

Top-level domain – The segment of an internet domain name that comes after the full stop. An example would be the top-level domains for different countries, all of which have two letters, such as .uk for the United Kingdom.

URL – Acronym for Uniform Resource Locator, which means a website's internet address. An example would be routledge.com/corporate/about-us.

User-generated content – Content created by non-professionals such as eyewitnesses or ordinary users of a web service. The term also goes by the abbreviation UGC.

Verification – The act of journalists' establishing the veracity of statements or media content.[7]

Notes

1 Kjell-Olav Hovde & Sigmund Grønmo, *Algorithm [Algoritme]* (18 May 2020). Retrieved 8 September 2020 from Store norske leksikon snl.no/algoritme

2 Ferrara et al., *The rise of social bots* (June 2016). Retrieved 10 September 2020 from Association for Computing Machinery doi.org/10.1145/2818717

3 Store norske leksikon, *Disinformation [Desinformasjon]* (15 June 2020). Retrieved 8 September 2020 from Store norske leksikon snl.no/desinformasjon
Claire Wardle & Hossein Derakhshan, *Information Disorder: Toward an interdisciplinary framework for research and policy making* (27 September 2017). Retrieved 8 September 2020 from The Council of Europe rm.coe.int/information-disorder-toward-an-interdisciplinary-framework-for-researc/168076277c

4 Ibid.

5 Bente Kalsnes, *Fake news [Falske nyheter]* (2019). Cappelen Damm Akademisk, p. 35.

6 Claire Wardle & Hossein Derakhshan, *Information Disorder: Toward an interdisciplinary framework for research and policy making* (27 September 2017). Retrieved 8 September 2020 from The Council of Europe rm.coe.int/information-disorder-toward-an-interdisciplinary-framework-for-researc/168076277c

7 Store norske leksikon, *Verify [Verifisere]* (20 August 2018). Retrieved 8 September 2020 from Store norske leksikon snl.no/verifisere

Index

Note: Page numbers in *italics* indicate figures on the corresponding pages.

For Product Safety Concerns and Information please contact our EU
representative GPSR@taylorandfrancis.com
Taylor & Francis Verlag GmbH, Kaufingerstraße 24, 80331 München, Germany

www.ingramcontent.com/pod-product-compliance
Lightning Source LLC
LaVergne TN
LVHW010923110826
845149LV00013B/2463

* 9 7 8 1 0 3 2 5 8 2 9 4 8 *